Unlocking THE VAULT

A Collection of Poetry and Prose

JOSEPH DEEHAN

Copyright © 2025 Joseph Deehan.

All rights reserved. No part of this book may be reproduced, stored, or transmitted by any means—whether auditory, graphic, mechanical, or electronic—without written permission of both publisher and author, except in the case of brief excerpts used in critical articles and reviews. Unauthorized reproduction of any part of this work is illegal and is punishable by law.

ISBN: 979-8-89419-745-6 (sc)
ISBN: 979-8-89419-746-3 (hc)
ISBN: 979-8-89419-747-0 (e)

Because of the dynamic nature of the Internet, any web addresses or links contained in this book may have changed since publication and may no longer be valid. The views expressed in this work are solely those of the author and do not necessarily reflect the views of the publisher, and the publisher hereby disclaims any responsibility for them.

One Galleria Blvd., Suite 1900, Metairie, LA 70001
(504) 702-6708

Dedicated to

Anna Deehan
Jenifer Dunbar
Joseph J. Deehan
Bridget Lundgren
Shawn Duffy
and some who are now gone,
Mary Ellen Deehan
Michael "Joe" Deehan
Mary Anne Hunt Deehan

Acknowledgments

To Arthur McMaster who edited the poetry of this volume and to Marcia Moston who edited the prose works. To Judith Chandler who, over several years, has reviewed much of the work in this volume. With their constructive insight, they have helped me bring out the most of whatever creative ability I may have. To Joe Carey for his helpful input on *Departure*. Finally, to the OLLI program and its staff at Furman University where some fifteen years ago by chance I registered for a poetry writing class. It changed the direction of my life.

Back Cover photo – Tommy Ennis
Curry's Cottage Tea Room photo – Kay O'Keefe
Self-Portrait with Bandaged Ear image – Public Domain
To Forgive Is Divine photo – Alamy Inc.
All other photos are from the Author's collection.

Contents

PART 1: POETRY

One Cedar Box 3
In Flight 4
Sleepless in the Battle 5
Yard Work 6
Wave Action 8
Garden State of Mind 9
At the Mall 10
Write on! 11
Black and White on a Wall 12
Night Light 13
The Dark Room 14
Roots 15
Sea Girt 16
Something Left Behind 17
Curry's Cottage Tea Room 18
Avignon 19
Autumn Abstraction 20
Sea Marsh 21
Hummingbirds 22
Wild Horses 23
Beyond the Pose 24
The Color Wheel (Pantoum) 25
Benbulben 26
View from Salt Life Deck 27
Spring Blur (American Sonnet) 28
The Polo Grounds 29

PART 2: POETRY CONTINUED

In Repose 33
Rebirth (Sonnet) 34

Killary Harbour 35
Self-Portrait with Bandaged Ear
    Vincent van Gogh 1889 36
The Fords 37
A Changing Tune (Sonnet) 38
Journey 39
Ode to a Eucalyptus 40
Clew Bay 41
The Cloud 42
Trapped in Rhyme – He 43
Trapped in Rhyme – She 44
John Ennis 45
In Search of the Words (American Sonnet) 47
Indelible 48
Thanksgiving Bounty 49
Ouch! 50
The Sea 51
The Night They Drove the Dixies Down 52
The Brogue 54
Autumn Leaves (Sonnet) 55
Downsizing 56
Summer Haiku 57

PART 3: POETRY CONCLUDED

Committal 61
Rainy Day 62
The Visitor 63
The Deep Unknown 64
Singer Island, February 19, 2019 66
A Noble Foe 67
The Looking Glass (Prose Poem) 68
Hidden Majesty 69
Dream On (Sonnet) 70
A New Perspective 71
The Abyss 72

Spring Break (Triolet). 73
Old Friend. 74
Turtle 75
What Went Wrong?. 76
The Pub. 77
At the Traffic Light 78
The White Shirt 79
The Quest. 80
At the Library. 81
The Flowers of Spring 82
Boarded Up. 83
'Tis the Season (Cinquain) 85
Reflection. 86
Winter Haiku 87

PART 4: PROSE FICTION

Lost Ball 91
The Red Convertible. 104
Departure. 108
Windfall 119
Genesis. 124
Help Wanted!. 126

PART 5: PROSE NON-FICTION

Summer 1960. 131
The Airplane Passenger 138
The Power of Inference 140
The Concert 143
Hibbing, MN. 147
The Thanksgiving Day Race 148
To Forgive Is Divine 151

PART 1

POETRY

One Cedar Box

rests on a broad oak stump,
a brown box of cedar construct
in the company of two photos—
one of a smiling white-haired man,
the other of a young boy with a baseball glove,
wearing a quizzical look on his face.

Seven decades separate the photos.
   Growing
      Learning
         Loving
            Marrying
               Working
                   Raising children
                       Doting on grandchildren
                           Helping the less fortunate
All are crowded into the small box.

People gather about, talk in soft tones
and smile with remembrance
of their times with him,
all those moments contained in the box.

He was a strong man,
quite athletic in his youth
and more than capable on a golf course
when he aged,
his strength and power
now dissipated among the ashes.

A tall man attired in a black suit
speaks prayerful words in monotone
and with stealth movement opens the box.

Wind scatters a life across the land.
Shoots of wild daffodils break the surface.

In Flight

These words I write today...
see them fly or sail away.

Some land in towns I do not know.
Others disembark on far off shores.
The words escape from printed pages
and find a path into unencumbered minds.

New thoughts, they furtively unlock
in distant brains I've never scanned.
Emotion flows down a soft young cheek.
Chuckles spring from tickling barbs.

Odd lines of verse birth reflections.
Look! They cut into a lonely soul.
Others scratch itches of whimsy and fantasy
that lay beneath the surface.

Whether they accomplish a mission
or induce a languorous afternoon nap,
a long rest on dusty shelves ensues...
such faithful friends, their work ends.

But new words I spawn tomorrow,
let them dig for gold or unearth sorrow.

Sleepless in the Battle

Come sleep, sweet sleep, the certain balm of peace.
These shards of guilt invade my space at night.
They dart and slash with random stabs of pain.
It's when my conscience tears apart the shield
of greed's deep need for wealth that drives my day.

Come sleep, sweet sleep, the certain balm of peace.
Oh guilt, dark guilt, please leave with haste. Be gone!
Don't scrape away the remnants of my soul.
I will repent, bring charity to bear,
and cleanse transgressions of self-centered ways.

Come sleep, sweet sleep, the certain balm of peace.
This day was spent absorbed in selfish toil
advancing goals to gild my bank account
and short another soul who's rightly due.
I tremble with how shallow I've become.

Come sleep, sweet sleep, the certain balm of peace.

Yard Work

A squall descended. It was so sudden...
to see his life end with that fluid twirl.
An unexpected loss hit me. That morning
I had chased him and his cohorts, with playful intent.

All worry free, with ample feed in the yard
and no clouds apparent on their horizon.
She gave no warning, picking him up by the neck
and swinging him 'round in the air

with the grace and precision of a matador.
My aging Grandmother, white haired and stooped,
snapped his neck on the second pass,
then looked at me with her impish grin.

Never in my brief time with that gentle woman
had I seen a sign of the assassin.
She had told Mom and Dad we would
have chicken for evening supper and said,

"Joey, come with me."
I had followed her into the yard, unaware
and unsuspecting of any murderous intent.
It was over so quickly, so shockingly.

Quietly I sat at the kitchen table
as they talked, unaffected by the back yard killing.
My mate of that morning
lay before me on the plate, naked and boiled.

How could I have any appetite?
Others devoured him without pause, as though
he had come packaged from the A&P market.
Now I understood the working of the food chain.

I left the table and walked to the window.
A solitary horse stood in the field.
He stared at me, the sun setting behind him and
my being now laden with a new awareness.

Author with Grandmother Bridget Hunt,
Doocastle, County Mayo Summer 1960

Wave Action

The waves roll on top of the sea
and end with a crash on the shore.
Over and over...I cannot break free
from the grasp they have on my core.

My gaze is fixed on their rhythmic advance,
my ears attuned to their steady beat.
I'm trapped in a peaceful trance,
content to watch them repeat.

Garden State of Mind

Newark, East Orange, Patterson, Passaic,
Jersey City, Hoboken, Elizabeth, Harrison,
Trenton, Camden.
Grey buildings, grey streets, grey smoke,
grey clouds.
Gardens without care, spent in the Garden State.
The Turnpike flows.

Sea Girt, Neptune, Belmar, Manasquan,
Point Pleasant, Bradley Beach, Asbury Park,
Seaside Heights, Wildwood.
Summer sand, splintered boards, crashing waves,
cotton candy, sunburn, rocking chairs, seaside air.
The respite ends...back to school.
The Parkway balks with congestion.

Short Hills, Llewelyan Park, Bedminster, Madison,
Mendham, Rumson, Far Hills.
Manicured lawns, private clubs, polo chucks.
Ride the train to NYC. Money talks.
Bring it back in neat green stacks.
Markets stall in the crystal ball.
The Tunnel clogs.

Blend it all in a mixing bowl—
a layered cake, iced to tempt.

Cut a piece—over nine million servings,
a taste for all.

At the Mall

They're all around.
Styles abound.
Short bob, straight line,
long bangs, asymmetrical.
Geometry infusion.
It's so cool to be cool.
Strut your stuff.
Nieman Marcus, Saks Fifth Avenue,
upscale chic, stylish streak
surrounds.
Cut those jeans, bloody knees.
Feel the pain.

Prada, Louis Vuitton.
Kate Spade.
It's in the bag.
Coach to win.
Cartier, Tiffany,
Ring it in. Sing their song,
Peel the carats,
boil the mix.
Cut those jeans, bloody knees.
Here we go with the grain.

Chanel, Dior.
It's in the air—Spring has sprung.
Click those heels, Nordstrum beat.
See the sheen,
time to preen.
Six-dollar frappe, the Grande's grand.
Barista nods, not so tall.
Cut those jeans, bloody knees.
Stitch the brain.
Again. Again.

Write on!

How many poems?
One hundred million?
One hundred billion?
Written over thousands of years...
every conceivable happening...
every conceivable feeling...
all expressed on poetic verse.
Write into the depth of night...of space...of time.

The nouveaux poet has written good poems...
has written bad poems.
I must write more, while there is still possibility.
Write into the depth of night...of space...of time.
I must write quickly...the words must flow.
Hurry or else
everything will have been written.
Write into the depth of night...of space...of time.
Write on! Write on!

Black and White on a Wall

The windows loom, bare of curtains or shades.
In front of the two-story State Bank of Commerce
stand four men wearing fedoras, dark jackets
with top button fastened and vests beneath,
white shirts secured at the collar,
two of them more formally set with ties.

Weeds break through the sidewalk at their feet.
A solitary fire hydrant stands sentry by a gaslight pole.
The grainy visages stare blankly
at the camera without expression,
as do those of three nearby shoeless boys
who wear rumpled grey shirts and dirt-stained pants.

One boy leans aimlessly against the building.
On the dirt side street an aged white horse
stands, fixed at head of a wagon,
next to him a man with a worn floppy hat.

A late 1800's scene filled with stolid faces
hangs on the wall. Perhaps due to
a photographer documenting town life, or
perhaps local businessmen seeking publicity.

What became of these subjects
after they quit the camera's gaze?
Were their lives filled with love
and fulfillment?
Or did misery and hardship capture their being?
Did they pass on wisdom and purpose that filtered
to descendants of today?

I reflect on such things while images stare at me
more than a century after a photographer memorialized
their existence. Here I sit on this same
Hendersonville Street.
Is it their progeny I see walk by?

Night Light

My thoughts of worry incessant,
I gaze at the silver moon crescent
amidst the sparkle of star-filled sky.

The wonder of nature, an anti-depressant,
my anxiety softens, I'm now fluorescent
as my soul embraces Glory on high.

The Dark Room

Darkness pervades the room
except for the solitary shaft of light
that pierces a tear in the
ragged window curtain.

The invading beam passes through a
cob web on its way to the empty
Smirnoff bottle on the floor.
The cabin creaks in the wind

for the boards that form it
are aged with ripened decay...only
rusted nail pimples holding them together.
The spiritless walls, which last breathed

fresh paint decades ago,
wrap themselves around my body
and mind. This world
cloisters my being.

Walking out the door seems an option,
but for what purpose?
Lying in this springless bed
with unwashed sheets is my existence.

I think about nothing for a time
but continue to look at the bottle
which scowls at me.
Is it God or the Devil who

transmits the sliver of light?
An unknown spirit looms.
No one can sew the curtain.
I rip it from the window.

Roots

I trod the green field,
my hand secured in Grandmother's
as she places the food pail
before the stolid cow.

The fields meander in all directions
and veil the boglands
containing decayed bones
from generations past.

Culture shift cracks and resculpts
rural hope into streetwise edges
that scrape the soul within.
Past lost, grey pavement greets my step.

Author with Grandmother Bridget Hunt
Doocastle, County Mayo 1947

Sea Girt

Dunes grasses bend
into ocean winds, as surf
pounds the shore, again and again,
relentless in its assault.

How many millions of years
has the pattern repeated,
nature never tiring in its insistent role?
Billions of grains of sand lie before me
wrapped in peace of past millennia,
holding the grasses in place.

All pieces play their part
and carry on with dutiful purpose.
I see the Majesty in this presentation
and hear His word muffled
in the sound of the foaming surf.
The truth of nature's essence
binds me in its serenity.

Something Left Behind

Unexpectedly, I find blond strands.
They push me back in time.
Months pass and connections fade.

Back then, after a day of thorough house cleaning,
I would find them—multiple batches of his hair
along the floor on the next morning.

His hair confronted me in a never-ending battle.
The broom, the Swifter, the vacuum cleaner—
each had its chance to enter the fray in defense
against the always shedding Labrador.

These few strands bring back lost moments.
I no longer see the tail wagging
or the anticipation in his yellow-rimmed eyes,
knowing there would be a treat.

I never understood the big deal
in scratching his belly.
Just lying on his back with legs in the air,
it seemed like life's ultimate comfort pleasure.

Scenes of Chipper romping with buddies,
splashing with them in Terry Creek,
snatching one of their dog park toys.
They all flash through my mind.

What power there is in
some hidden strands.
Most loyal friend, rest peacefully
in your bookshelf coffin.

Curry's Cottage Tea Room

From my small table, snug against the wall
I peer through the nine-pane window onto
a few people ambling along James Street.
Gentle rain falls on Westport as it awakens.

Mrs. Curry walks to the window,
steps on her chair, and opens a latched transom.
The cool morning air jolts my senses to life. Yes,
Ireland is present. The lilt of spoken word embraces.

The morning adamantly calls for the *Full Irish*.
I order two eggs sunny side up, streaky bacon,
sausage, fried potatoes, brown bread with butter,
and add adventure with some black pudding.

Mrs. Curry's breakfast propels me toward the day
with exhilarated anticipation of trekking Connemara
and its mysterious sheep laden, green mountains.
Ireland runs deep, and even deeper.
I hear the fiddles and the flutes.

Avignon

The medieval wall exudes a cold presence
as I walk through the open city gate on Rue Saint Charles.
With stone buildings and French signage
everything seems unreceptive.

A man stands with a young boy and dog at the corner.
The boy says "Papa" followed by
something foreign to my ear.
As the dog trots briskly toward me,
the boy yells some words in a stern voice.

The dog immediately turns back,
sits in obedience and receives a treat.
How inadequate am I when a dog's fluency
in French surpasses mine!

The immensity of Palais des Papes overwhelms
the nearby shops and restaurants.
The foreboding Gothic walls stare with contempt.
What forces drove the Popes from Rome
to this small city for almost 70 years?
I imagine something beyond boredom with pasta.

The rattling trill of cirl buntings deflects my attention.
Laughing children riding wooden horses
circle about with glee
on the Menage Pour Enfants merry-go-round.
Their French is a language I understand.

I divert to O'Neill's Irish Pub
on Boulevard Saint Raspail for a Guiness.
The black brew softens the austerity
of the medieval city ramparts,
now not so ominous.

I ponder whether I should study French—
and take another sip.

Autumn Abstraction

Woven with threads of subtle brown,
spirited reds and joyous golds abound.
A Carolina mountain sports its haughty crown.

Energy flows from nature's bold display.
I slide a brush atop the palette's scape
and coat vibrant hope across my day.

But the world revolves and daily blows pierce
the veneer. Hope decays with life's jabs and fears.
Sun dims its light, then disappears.

In dystopian wind, trees bend and lurch
and I join the lost who daub in futile search.
Leaves fall to wizen and die on blackened earth.

Sea Marsh

The afternoon sun sheds its cloud cover
and lights the sedge, standing at attention.
Time moves slowly through Hilton Head marsh.

Wax myrtles and palmettos with their thatch skirts
guard the marsh's western border
while sand dunes rise above on ocean side.

The outgoing tide retreats toward the sea
exposing abundance of life
amid grass shoals and mud banks.

Herons sit atop a red cedar
in anticipation of their evening meal.
Not prone to waiting,

egrets flock in and settle among the sedge,
their sustenance hunt beginning.
Mud fiddlers, oysters and periwinkles abound,

unknowing of the impending danger.
Nature's ecosystem works its daily magic,
not in any rush...everything in its time.

Hummingbirds

They're such a colorful lot,
   the blue throated, the cinnamon, the ruby throated...
   and oh, so industrious.

I miss them.
   It's the way they hover...like helicopters
     in front of the feeder...
       wings lost in a blur.

I miss them
   and wonder where they are.
     Perhaps they've flown to a feeder
       in someone else's poem.

If only he hadn't come,
   a thief in the night.
     A black iron pole stands in solitude.

I wish they would fly back
   and lose themselves in my word maze,
     while a bear sleeps comfortably in the woods.

Wild Horses

The rising sun pours the cacophonic beat
of hooves onto the mesa.
They power across the plain atop a bluff,
untethered by man,
free as the north wind.

The golden leads in majesty––gleaming
against the western Dakota sky,
exuberant and unafraid.
He signals an ease in movement
and they slowly patrol the high grasses,
taking their fill.

The young black colt has no patience.
Running is his want.
The leader will not be rushed.
An appaloosa mare nudges the young one
who finds peace in the grass.
Streams of satisfaction flow nearby.

The silence of the open land envelops all
in an equine bond of unity.
Nothing is spoken
but the golden's spirit descends over the herd
and strong legs flash across the plain,
free as the north wind.
They disappear into the sun.

Beyond the Pose

His dark hair is parted and slicked back.
The suit and tie he wears on the photo
makes the immigrant laborer
look like a young banker.

Deep into the image in sepia tones,
beyond the paper on which it lays,
I peer into the mind
behind the eyes that resemble mine.

"I'll show them back in Sligo
how well I'm doing in America.
I'll be a success in this country.
The decision to leave was mine...was right,
no guilt, no need for them to know the suit is borrowed."

I see his determination.
The courage to cross a vast ocean,
to live in an unknown land
where he would father a yet to be known son.

I look deeper into an almost century old photo
and see the grandchildren he barely knew as infants.
His great-grandchildren were mist of angels in his time.
One day they will mine the depths of this photo
and wonder what might have been,
if an eighteen-year-old had gone a different way.

The Color Wheel (Pantoum)

Buds emerge and give birth to Spring anew.
The grey of Winter's past now disappears.
My spirit soars as new delights accrue.
Encumbrances in life seem less severe.

The grey of Winter's past now disappears.
I frolic in the joy of sun's embrace.
Encumbrances in life seem less severe.
I'm thankful for the bounty of God's grace.

I frolic in the joy of sun's embrace.
But colors fade and leaves drop to the ground.
I'm thankful for the bounty of God's grace.
The color wheel seeds life as it goes 'round.

But colors fade and leaves drop to the ground.
My spirit soars as new delights accrue.
The color wheel seeds life as it goes 'round.
Buds emerge and give birth to Spring anew.

Benbulben

In Drumcliffe graveyard one stone stands apart,
only a few yards from the doors of the church
at which his great-grandfather served as rector.
Yeats lies peacefully as the tourists pause
and ponder the words engraved.

Cast a cold eye
On life, on death.

The raised plateau of Benbulben sits atop
the steel grey walls and sloping green fields.
Lyrical shadows skip across the mountain
as it peers toward the ancient church yard
where its hagiographer rests.

The sun slips furtively between the clouds
and then falls beyond Sligo Bay.
The dark of night drives all away
and verse sounds softly in the yard.
Neighbors hear his words with murmuring affirmation.

Horseman, pass by!

View from Salt Life Deck

A gull flies over Amelia Island's sands
high above the rolling tide.
I detect no underlying scheme or plan
behind its effortless thermal ride.

Its head is fixed with steady gaze below
as though conducting some weighty exam.
What draws such attention in this avian show...
perhaps a sleeping oyster or idle clam?

Spring Blur
(American Sonnet)

Bud busting cherry blossoms cast a pink hue
that steeps within my temperament.
Poplars, oaks, birch break the grey stick panorama
with subtle shows of green.

My foe, the bone cutting north wind
has disappeared from morning walks,
with Terry Creek's chilled rush overtaken
by gurgling swills of imagination.
Tufts of enthused fescue erupt nearby.

In the midst of a pleasant Spring photo
it lurks, hidden among the newborn.
My throat sounds crackling falsetto notes
as back and forth Kleenex fly.
With a chartreuse pallor my car yields a sigh.

The Polo Grounds

Upper Manhattan buildings fallen grey
and foreboding exude cold indifference
to our presence.
I walked alongside my father
who confidently told me, several times,
we were almost there.
Fragments pop up, then disappear. Lock 'em in here.

We turn a corner and I see
people converging a block away.
There it is––the Polo Grounds.
Soon we are part of the crowd on a ramp
leading us to a concourse within the ballpark.

The structure imposes its presence,
a darker gray than the stoic buildings around...
alive and pulsing.
Need order now. Get each part in a row.

My heart starts to race.
What ten-year-old boy wouldn't be excited
going to his first Major League Baseball game!
A night game no less!
To see Willie Mays!

The noise level intensifies
with streams of people
heading to concession stands or toward their seats.
They course in various directions
as though blood vessels giving life
to this concrete city structure.
How do I know? So long ago.

Then I see it––
illuminated by beaming lights
on the roof top stanchions,
a brilliant green field,
the soul of the Polo Grounds.
I stare in awe.
It's all so near. The color's clear.

The manicured green grass of the outfield
excites me. Color so vivid,
a shade I didn't know existed.
The infield perfectly cut––no jagged edges––
no rocks or clods––just smoothly rolled brown dirt
set against the green grass.

This is not the rough baseball diamond
I play on at Branch Brook Park.
A real Major League stadium stares at me!
When I see the Giants run onto the field
to start the game, happiness explodes...
actual Major League baseball players before my eyes.

They laugh. They cry. Just like you and I.
All in place now,
the pieces retrieved from the memory vault
form the mosaic of that night––
thousands and thousands ago––
clearer, more refreshing than most.
It happened.
So I believe.

PART 2

POETRY CONTINUED

In Repose

The willowy tasseled blades of grass,
of which you are not cognizant,
intrude on your gray bones that lie inert.
Your once beaming eyes are hollow and sightless,
their spectacles long smashed and scattered
as bits of eternity.

Your voice that would call out with authority
to clear your way has long been silent.
If only your owner had recorded your exploits
what stories could be told.
He'll never have the chance for he lies in the ground
out on McKinney Road.

Your wheels that spun with enthusiasm
as they carried you on those adventures
were the victims of time's amputation.
You now rest in dreary stupor on cinder blocks
while your once strong bones give way
to the cancer of rust.

How many cases of moonshine
did you transport to the speak-easies in town?
How many cops did you outrace as they chased you
through the back roads of the foothills?

You were once proud...proud of those feats
as well as the Sunday dirt track races you conquered.
A life worth recalling but one that is forgotten.
You wallow in a field of anonymity ignored,
like every blade of grass.

Rebirth (Sonnet)

The truth presents itself before my eyes
as waves beat twice against the silent shore
in rhythm with the seagulls' plaintive cries.
For proof of Majesty I need no more.

Oh yes, there's discord on horizon's edge.
Man's lust for wealth and power will disrupt,
but man is just a toad among marsh sedge
with limits born and often too corrupt.

While mayhem rules upon our cities' streets
and wars produce catastrophic ruin,
We know each year the birth of Spring repeats
in bringing forth once more new buds to bloom.

With God's abiding love, the Earth renews—
so man still has a chance the path to choose.

Killary Harbour

A country surrounded by sea-lapped shore—
its many broad bays invade the coast
at Bantry, Galway, Sligo and more—
but you maintain a lonely post.

Glaciers formed your entry, long and narrow,
flowing into tiny Leenane
with its lurking gulls and chirping sparrows.
You stand alone in all the land.

Skinny runt among all the bays—
you deal with peers' disdain, so untoward,
while completing dutiful ebbs and rises unfazed.
How does it feel to be Ireland's only fjord?

Self-Portrait with Bandaged Ear
Vincent van Gogh 1889

The Café closes and on the terrace
appear bottle ghosts.
Lights in the starry night sky darken.
Irises wilt in the field.
Thunder echoes in your ear
and reality departs without farewell.
The slap of the razor on the leather strop
sounds a mesmerizing beat.

The Fords

Albertha Ford, died 1945, age three years, one month
Abraham Ford, died 1944, age one year, one month
Eddie Ford, died 1944, age six months

Small gravestones snuggle three abreast
in a humble, ungated cemetery.
Large oaks, draped with sorrowful strands of Spanish moss,
stand as sentries overlooking the infant remains.
Rebecca Ford (1925 – 1980) rests directly behind
the three weathered stones in Union Cemetery.

In an isolated part of this barrier island
a mother lies, still protective of three small bodies
she couldn't save in life.
What dreams did a poor black mother have for her children—
dreams crushed before those children
could have dreams of their own?

A breeze carries evanescent vapors through
the latent moss hangings.
Images of deep sorrow in the Ford household
some seventy-five years earlier shroud my mind.
With head bowed, I turn and walk
down the dirt path wondering *why*.

A Changing Tune (Sonnet)

Aretha wails a soulful plea of love.
I spar with semis in the six-lane flow
through tank farms and grey vistas, bereft of
the Jersey vibe I felt so long ago.

Now decades gone, attuned to Southern ways,
the Blue Ridge Mountains pace my daily life
with pines and streams that form a verdant maze
of succor in a world so torn with strife.

For Newark streets were all I knew in youth
with wise guys chirping on tight city blocks.
They had an edge and spoke an urban truth,
so foreign now—I ponder, taking stock.

I know today I cannot make that run.
As Dylan sang, "May you stay forever young."

Journey

I saw the rose beneath the ground.
Deep in the earth the seed broke down.
Green shoots emerged and hurried toward the light.
I saw their struggle, resolution unbound--
they broke through, drawn to sun's birthing warmth.
The stems bore buds. With new energy, no sound,
a red rose burst forth.
It now lights the world around.
I saw the rose beneath the ground.

Ode to a Eucalyptus

Verdant companions once inspired,
Indeed, they fueled competitive desire
that drove you to dominance among your peers.
You stood proudly above them
but they are long gone, victims all––some from disease,
many at the hands of the Marriott assassin.

You now stoop––alone,
gnarled and twisted, bent with age.
The elixir sap of youth now drained
while emptiness and anguish filter from your roots
and feed your brittle heart,
warmth and joy long eroded aspects of your being.

Your horizontal black stare runs deep
as you capture me in your visage.
What drives your focus on me,
a lone visitor in this beachside parking lot?
What is it that you see?
Just a mirror reflection
of what you've come to be.

Clew Bay

I wander the road from Murrisk
and gaze at the twinkling of the sunlit water.
1600 years ago Patrick viewed this wonder
of God's creative genius from atop the Reek.

Amidst the pain and loneliness of his forty-day fast,
it fed him quiet solace
as he looked upon the rapturous encounter
of emerald slopes and sapphire sea.

On a buoyant spring morning
the scene intoxicates my senses.
It's there for all to see.
My faith rises from its slumber.
Those who look closely will awaken.

The Cloud

Forlorn cloud within the sky
don't turn grey and start to cry.
Stand aside and let the sun
cast its warmth on everyone.

Trapped in Rhyme – He

He had to write lines
for he couldn't mime.
Cheap little lines
with playschool rhyme
he wrote for thin dimes,
for he couldn't mime.
He never had time
to flush his mind,
rid thoughts that bind.
It was a grind,
no gold to mine,
no mountains to climb,
just cheap rhyme,
what a decline!
He liked to fine dine,
picked teeth with old tines,
washed down with cheap wine
from street hustled vines.
Oh, they maligned
and put him in line
with the swine
in their slime
and their grime.
That made him whine.
But they were all blind
so there was no crime.
It was so unkind
for he could not find
days with sunshine,
and he still couldn't mime.
Oh, how he did pine
for that T'bird filled stein.

Trapped in Rhyme – She

She hit the sand
with tan and glam,
a bit flim-flam.
Sought shallow fans
who looked and scanned.
They gave her a hand.
That's how it began.
Rocked with the band,
an all-night stand.
It was all a scam,
a trashcan plan
to get honey ham
and sugared yams
followed by flan.
But the sham hit the fan
with scowling Spam
in a greasy pan.
Told her to scram.
No one lent a hand
or gave a sweet damn.
Damaged young lamb
fled in a tin can sedan
across vast empty land
with just an engram.

John Ennis

Freshman English—Frost, Sandburg.
A little foreign, but the Math comfort zone
follows an Arithmetic medal at SRL,
Acing Algebra is pure. Numbers, logic—so true.

Second year—I expect the same.
Algebra II with Brother Kavanaugh continues strong.
A wrinkle enters English Lit. II with John Ennis.
He introduces Wordsworth, Keats, Byron, and more.

Sure, Pip and Mrs. Haversham complicate a bit
but I get used to riding the rails
into Mr. Ennis' *great expectations*.
"She walks in Beauty, like the night
Of cloudless climes and starry skies:"
Wow! Pictures do spring from words.

I hear, "Sit up Mr. Deehan. No slouching."
To raise myself from a lazy teenage sitting posture
I pull the front edge of the desktop.
Without malicious intent, I rip it from its frame.

"Joseph, Joseph. Please sit erectly without theatrics,"
a faint smirk of exasperation on Mr. Ennis' face.
I apologize, red faced and surely headed to Jug later
under the watch of menacing Brother Kelly.

Mr. Ennis finishes the day's class with discussion on Yeats.
Anticipated punishment never arrives.
No Jug, not a harsh word...
unexpected mercy.
Was this the true *second coming*?

Some months later I stand
in a small church graveyard in Drumcliff, Sligo, Ireland
and read these words on a grey tombstone.
"Cast a cold eye on life, on death. Horseman pass by."
What did Yeats mean?

John Ennis was a sower of seeds
that he scattered among his students. Decades fade...
one latent seed in a retired CPA's fallow soul
blossoms into an avocation of writing verse.

Burn bright, burn bright
and expose worlds of new delight.

In Search of the Words
(American Sonnet)

The plane lifts from Houston Intercontinental.
City buildings draw farther away,
now pieces of a child's model train set.
The paperback slips from my hands.
We rise steadily to join my mind in the clouds,
where I swirl with disbelief and fear.
No...not fear, a mindset closer to cutting inadequacy.
How will I tell them? Is there a way I can escape?
Disembodied...no pain if we crash...
but this plane will surely land at BWI.
Medical skills so certain to make everything right.
What words can fill the abyss for three young children,
soon to learn of her death at a faraway hospital?
Four decades later, I search for the person on that flight.

Indelible

He was born free, but needed help.
Free as a bird,
he flew into his mother's arms.

He was born free, but couldn't talk.
He chirped into his mother's ear
and she danced to his tune.

Small and helpless he grew through her love.
Dependent though he was,
he didn't know fear for she was fearless.

On a long-ago day she made him tall
when she lifted him high and he rapped
the brass knocker on the Doocastle door.

Feeling comfort in the nest of her arms,
he rapped with joy as her smile grew
through the pride in her three-year-old.

Seven decades later the moment returns.
Rapping the door knocker at that Ireland farmhouse,
memory draped in cobwebs, clings to the recesses.
The joy of a mother's love burns brightly.

Thanksgiving Bounty

The annual family Thanksgiving gathering,
calendar item to look forward to,
routines and menu repeated,
conversation familiar,
convivial, humorous,
brightness abounds.
People now gone,
memories remain,
phosphorescent,
gilded lore,
comforting,
gossamer,
mystical,
fading.

Ouch!

Found the devil?
Don't start to revel
Buyer beware
The Russian Bear stares

Politics sought
Politics fraught
Fulfill bent desire
Leave progeny mired

Unleashed anger
Look for the danger
Marxism boils
Unglued cities roil

Hate on a spike
All must think alike
Young bears being groomed
Foreshadow the doom

Socialism's steady creep
Grandchildren will weep

The Sea

Jellyfish stranded by the vanishing tide—
sea gulls peck freely for sustenance.
The birds' indifference to my presence comforts.
Like them I belong to the sea.

I am drawn...drawn by assurances
of the waves sounding on the shore.
My strokes measured and rhythmic,
in sync with the steady beat of the surf.

The flow of currents I cannot feel,
the horizon distant but lurking
with the unknown of beyond
and mystery of unmeasured depths.

The swimming becomes effortless.
A swimmer's high clears my psyche––
no strain, no life stress, mind unblemished.
Pulses of verse invade my being.

Words tumble freely about my head
and meld into cohesive meter
with the tang of inviting rhyme.
All secure in my mind.

With no rudder to guide
I will follow where led.
The horizon comes ever closer—
no barriers, no limits.

Carried by the wind
vapors of sand travel to the sea,
each grain unknowing of its destination
but certain to find a place.

The Night They Drove the Dixies Down

They lie in a dark drawer
beside the Stars and Bars.
The Chicks are the Chicks—no more, but less.
They're not whistling Dixie anymore.

Stonewall's cast iron image stares at black tarpaulin,
no views of VMI available.
Robert Lee not announcing the UVA football game—
Richmond's Monument Avenue almost naked.

The culture erasers blitz the South
with all the vengeance of Sherman,
remains discarded.
Phantom Pink Pearls finish what he started.

Lincoln killed again in 2020.
There's room in the drawer for you, Abe,
but it is getting crowded.
Atticus Finch and Huck Finn lie nearby.

But not just the South.
Their tentacles stretch, almost unending.
A long dead Greek, Homer, discarded
in the drawer without much fanfare.

But there never is.
It's just accepted, weakness flows.
Mao casts admiring glances.
His methods brutal, but hardly more effective.

We'll try healing once again.
A different methodology this time, Abe.
You know—keeping up with the new ways.
Just nestle alongside George, Thomas, Andrew, et al.

Uniformity of thought strikes the anvil
and sparks singe all within range.
Librarians move Orwell from Fiction shelves
to History/Current Events.

Yes Abe, we'll all have scars from our journey
to the world of Ultimate Outlook.
Erasure marks only hurt for a while—
so they tell us.

Que sera, sera.

The Brogue

I pass the ten euro note to the smiling cashier
in payment for a few groceries.
The tonal inflection of the greeting strikes me.
"How are ye dis fine summer mornin'?" she asks.

The lilt of her brogue rises in just the right spot,
as though part of a sung verse.
The melodic sound of Irish speech sets well
on the tongues of the people in this lyrical land.

With good cheer she hands me some change.
A song thrush alights from a fiddle
as she raises it to her shoulder.
My foot starts tapping.

Autumn Leaves (Sonnet)

I now recall—it wasn't long ago.
Their birth occurred in time of grey malaise
when hope was scant and spirits ebbed and flowed.
The land presented only gloomy days.

But they emerged and burst upon the scene.
They grew and flourished, filling a great void.
The trees that bore them, painted brilliant green,
all traces of past winter then destroyed.

Through summer, forests wore majestic dress,
impressing all who gazed at mountain's crown.
When autumn chill brought change and sweet duress,
the leaves aflame bore coats of red and brown.

In silent prayer they fell without a sound.
Now autumn leaves lie dead on hardened ground.

Downsizing

One green onyx vase, striated with muted brown,
stands on the middle shelf, devoid of flowers to brighten...
its only neighbor, a dark walnut box, dust laden.

The shelves above and below straighten with emptiness.
All books lie silenced, one atop another, in moving boxes,
ready to journey in a rite of passage––downsizing.

The walnut box reposes full, heavy in an unsuspecting way.
Too heavy for a shelf in the new house?
If I lighten the box, I lighten the past.

What should I remove?
His chase of Rosie across the field in pursuit of her stick...
the theft of Bailey's tennis ball...his belly flop splash in the creek...

the scamper to an interior room at the first crack of thunder...
or his quizzical look when she entered in white coat
as I bade a final goodbye, trying to avert eye contact.

Heavy indeed, but the new house will have to bear the weight.
I wipe the walnut box with a compliant dust cloth.

Summer Haiku

Morning sun rolls on.
Oppressive heat fills the day.
Thunderclouds open.

Sun blasts without pause.
Power outages ensue.
Longing for AC.

Summer beat goes on.
Humidity blankets all.
Shade tree oasis.

Heat driven drought rules.
Water restrictions abound.
Vibrant lawns turn brown.

Dusk arrives late on
a languorous summer day.
Fireflies light the night.

PART 3

POETRY CONCLUDED

Committal

Young children, on recess in the schoolyard,
play with enthusiasm unleashed
during their break from classes.
I listen to the prayerful words of the priest.
Bob would have enjoyed the background sounds
of laughter and glee.

The playful notes contrast with the solemnity
of Bob's committal.
Committal—that's what the priest calls it—
none can be stronger.
Following the prayers, a woman opens the niche
and places the gray box containing Bob's dust inside.

The last echo sounding in the niche
comes from schoolyard exuberance.
She closes and locks it.
Bob is fully committed—an eternity
inside the small walls.
Of course, prayer calls for a higher end.

The priest speaks a few words with family members.
Dispersion follows.
The children's sounds surround
Bob in the niche—
joyful music
for his eternal listening.

Rainy Day

The rhythm of the falling rain
adds tempered beat to each refrain,
while I sit alone at home
and read a gentle flowing poem.

For when I sit alone at home
a poem makes me feel not so alone
as I look at the window pane
and see the rhythm of the falling rain.

The Visitor

Unknown to us, he sneaks in
without announcing his presence,
a thief slowly carrying out
his torment under cover
of feigned normality.

Little things, seeming reticent
to show their presence.
Her voice a little more difficult to hear,
her handwriting starting to
shrink in size.

Over time, other annoyances surface.
Her once confident walking stride
now reduced to a diffident shuffle,
her balance a little wobbly.
We took it for granted,

just a natural part of aging.
All gradual, no reason for alarm.
The robber doesn't bother
with formal introductions.
He's so damn sneaky.

When he blows his cover with
intensified symptoms,
you realize you're stuck with him.
The therapy fends as best it can.
The meds keep him at a bit of distance.

But there is no end to it.
The obstructions to ordered life
are rooted like oaks.
While once a casual visitor,
Mr. Parkinson refuses to leave.

The Deep Unknown

He would leave the two-room schoolhouse
and walk a mile to the rock-walled green field,
the sheep his companions for the next few hours.
A small stone house with his parents
and eight siblings awaited at days end.

An existence that could not support a future,
seemingly hopeless but clinging to a vision.
At eighteen he crossed the great ocean for
a new world where a dream might become reality.
From rural farmland to the streets of New Jersey.

What was the depth of his frustration with life in Ireland?
What future did he foresee in America?
What were his fears disembarking at Ellis Island and
coping with the newness of urban life?
What challenges did he face? What demons?

Many questions without answers.
My father never talked much about his youth
in Ireland or his early years in America.
I never asked, being caught up in my own world
of friends and school and sports.

Some insight came when I was sixteen
on a summer trip to Ireland with my parents.
A moment of intense feeling surfaced
at the house of my father's brother,
the sole sibling who had remained in Ireland.

That day he saw his mother, then bedridden,
for the first time in 39 years. He broke down
when they embraced, releasing his past.
I had never seen my father cry.
Two months later my grandmother died.

That was a time for me to probe
with questions about his youth and life journey.
I didn't...still too self-absorbed.
The questions about my father's inner being
in his youth remain unanswered.

A life proceeds and moments sink
into the past without fanfare.
The past forgotten,
the past never to be resurrected.
The present consumes us.

Not knowing the fears and hopes
that drove my father's youth leaves
a part of my being undiscovered.
And so it shall remain.
Rock-walled green fields encircle my mind.

Stone remains of Deehan house,
Glenavoo, Lough Talt, County Sligo

Singer Island, February 19, 2019

Super Moon! Super Moon!
You sing a joyful buoyant tune.
Glow on land. Glow on sea.
Shine your focused light
throughout ever brightening night.
Guide my path. Set me free.

A Noble Foe

I stand quietly with gaze fixed.
After three days of futility,
frustration has built into stress.
I relax my hand, ridding the
grip tension that would lessen
the speed of the upcoming strike.
Previous attempts have resulted in failure.
A once flawless skill eroding with age?

Now perfectly still with weapon in hand
and nerves on edge stemming from prior misses,
I stare with purpose at the target,
perched on his threadlike legs.
My initial detestation has morphed
into admiration of its quickness
and instantaneous escapes.
Steady...
steady...
swish BAM!

With smash of the folded newspaper
my foe now lies there...squished.
There is no satisfaction. I may actually miss
the encounters with this fly,
whose only crime was an unending hunt
for organic decay. A tinge of sadness
surfaces as I discard the remains
into the trash.

The Looking Glass
(Prose Poem)

He stared out the window toward the parking lot, the cars standing perfectly still, each in the same parking spot as the day before, and the day before that. No motion, other than the leaves of the solitary oak, rustling with melancholy sways. On occasion a person, usually younger, would pass the window, the odd one might wave. He liked that. He wished they could say hello, but there was no conversation through the window.

He missed her so. This morning he was agitated because he couldn't remember whether it was three years ago or five. Damn memory, letting him down again. Whichever, it had been too long. Now and then, when looking out the window, he could see her faint reflection alongside his own. He would call her name. Once he pointed out her image to an aide. The aide replied it was just the shadow of the old tree. Some people are jerks and just can't see what's right before their eyes.

They didn't understand him as she could. Shortly, they would wheel him out to the dining area for another tasteless lunch, and he'd sit there eating in the midst of doddering people he didn't like. They didn't have any damn enthusiasm. She had always been enthusiastic about life…until….

The days were relentless, one upon another, each a carbon copy. Time was a sentence without punctuation. He saw the clouds rolling in. It would rain soon.

Hidden Majesty

It seems at times just beyond my grasp,
the link I seek to find His holy power.
Though I cannot see or touch, He must be there...
His manifestation behind the bloom of each new flower.

Dream On (Sonnet)

The barren field presents itself this day,
now ready for submission to the plough.
Life on the farm restricts with bars of gray,
but dreams alight and filter through the clouds.

The years in school have kept her dreams at bay.
With school behind, the future looms ahead.
Her dreams, once furtive, now are into play,
but rending ties fills a young heart with dread.

The dreams take form and turn into a plan.
Eye-welled departure from the farm precedes
a journey 'cross the sea to a new land,
there setting foot with grip on her prayer beads.

Now decades on, a poet looks above.
Beyond the clouds he sees a mother's love.

Author's mother, Mary Anne Hunt Deehan,
on left, Doocastle, County Mayo, 1935

A New Perspective

An invading white flotilla fills the sky,
its descent steady and unending.
The sight is new to him...
his locale normally hostile
to foreign forms of precipitation.

A freshly formed blanket covers lawn,
bushes and trees. With eyes fixated,
he enters this new world, unsure
of his next move. Wonder of the unknown
injects a serene stillness into his being.

His sniffs can't discern the usual scents.
Invigorated by the sensation of
cold white mystery, a joyful romp ensues.
When the newness wanes, he reverts to a
walking pace with random stops for relief.

A travel through wonder and buoyant fun
leads to peaceful satisfaction.
The exploration soon terminates.
A trail of yellow markers leaves
evidence of his snow adventure.

The Abyss

Bullets fly. Shoppers lie in pools of blood.
Bullets fly. Children die,
frozen by fear.
Grains of sand scatter in the winds of time
and disappear in the fading distance.

Innocents died, from fourth graders to octogenarians.
When they awoke that morning
did they perceive the shadow on their horizon?
Did they sense a time to prepare for the hereafter,
to ready their souls for eternity?
Some with lives barely begun,
all with lives incomplete.

Eighteen-year-olds armed for combat,
combat against non-combatants.
Eighteen-year-olds lost in the vortex
of the deepest black hole.
Buffalo, New York and Uvalde, Texas.
Seventeen hundred miles apart in distance
but related through bloodlines of nihilism.

A society produces beings not weighted with souls.
Families without structure,
entertainment without boundaries,
churches with empty pews,
social media with ease of entry into the nether world...
dark, absent all light.
The moral compass does not function.
The North Pole of humanity lies in ruin.

Spring Break (Triolet)

When Springtime hues of pink appear,
the vestiges of Winter cry.
Of stinging chill, I have no fear,
when Springtime hues of pink appear.
My spirits soar, my mind so clear.
Relief is here. I yield a sigh.
When Springtime hues of pink appear,
last vestiges of Winter die.

Old Friend

They carried you away,
dust covered, brown veneer,
tattooed with glass rings.
They dumped you in the back of a pickup.
You looked so alone as you left my possession...
left my life.

My first portal to the outside world,
The Shadow
   The Green Hornet
     The Lone Ranger
        Fibber Magee and Molly

I sat at your base more than seven decades past.
You also played those 78 rpm's...
sounds of Gene Autry, Bing Crosby and Kate Smith.
Now inoperable in a world devoid of vacuum tubes.

Oh, those long-ago nights
when I sat before you
enthralled at the sounds, the stories
that poured from you,
a magical machine.

A connection—my last to
that small apartment in Newark.
You bore Philco as a name.
Now gone, so old, as am I.
The past has now passed
for I watched them drive you away
along with my childhood world of make-believe.

Turtle

How cumbersome it is to live beneath a shell,
with its ever-present shadow, no matter where I dwell.
Many predators assume I'm such easy prey,
but the shield protects me each and every day.

They stare and wonder at my slow but steady gait.
I must find shelter or become a bobcat's bait.
I'll soon withdraw within my trusty lid
and from their hungry gaze I'll stay securely hid.

No need to chase down creatures with my feet
when grass and leaves are all I need to eat.
A turtle's day may seem a life of ease
but care and caution are my protective keys.

What Went Wrong?

They each had a mother—
I assume mothers who loved
and nurtured them as babes.
Along what straight line was there
a crooked turn?

Did their mothers hold and caress them
and watch them grow into boys,
believing they would become fine men?
What went wrong?

Did the boys lose sight of
the love in their mothers' eyes,
perhaps distracted by an aberrant
spirit from the netherworld?

At what point did they
snap the neck of the canary
in its cage before it flew?
Hitler...Stalin...Mao

How cruel to crush a mother's dream.

The Pub

Two dull windows flank a brown wooden door,
the slate roof topped by a smokeless chimney.
A few sparse trees border the empty gravel
parking ground. Green fields, populated only
with sheep, surround...filling the landscape.

In this rural setting the building, fixed in isolation,
carries no marrow of life...an innocuous empty structure.
When dusk begins to intrude, the first arrives, parking
near the entrance. In the ensuing moments
some additional souls enter the car park.
A couple arrives by bicycle on the country boreen.
More come over time...bees to the hive.

The building begins to breathe and slowly
stretches its frame. Laughter follows music
and song, pints flow. Vibrations of joy
overtake this singular place of community life.
The daytime dormant building has transformed
into the breathing pulse of the townland.

The pace of the banter eventually slows
and the depth of the night brings quiet
as souls disperse back among the darkened fields...
the community rejuvenated, now prepared
to deal with the following day.

At the Traffic Light

He stares at me with soulless eyes,
stubble covering a hollow, weathered face.
Although not threatening, his gaze
layers me with discomfort.

The crude cardboard sign states
a simple plea.
NEED MONEY FOR FOOD
His appearance conveys the need clearly,
the sign redundant.

Guilt weighs on my mind.
Should I give him $10 for a sandwich?
I rationalize. He'd spend the
money on a pint of liquor.

Freedom appears in a green light.
I accelerate, leaving with guilt intact.
If he used the money for booze,
it would be on him.

Never gave him the opportunity.
Now it's on me.

The White Shirt

lying on midnight black
pavement

the white shirt blood
red

cloth laden with jagged
holes

his eyes glazed in
terror

The Quest

The search begins…a word…a phrase.
I rack my brain, scraping the walls of the cavern.
Hidden from view, the concealment seemingly
intended, as though to increase my frustration.
I know they exist. I've traveled this road before.

Find the right words and you craft an image.
Keep at it and…
Shazam! Sometimes the image
is born in the form of a metaphor,
the Queen of all images.
Care for the metaphors. Cradle them
for they are the precious gold of poetry.

Link the images to create a magical excursion,
an excursion into the unknown.
Then, proceeding through the poem,
take the turn. Yes, a detour.
Surprise them with the volta.
For what is a poem without a volta but
just an ongoing ride on the highway,
one without an intriguing destination.

At the Library

Billions line the shelves...words, words,
and more words.
They're everywhere. I'm surrounded on all sides.
But I can't find any...any that will suit my need.

The problem presents itself.
I don't know my need.
What am I trying to say?
What should I write?

Which words will fit? Those that construct
the clear, terse narrative of Hemingway,
or those that lead the long, drawn out
obscurity of Faulkner?

The Muse has abandoned me.
I wander aimlessly through the aisles,
hoping some nearby author's thoughts
will vault via invisible waves into my head.

Oh, the frustration in this search for words.
There must be a phrase...a flash of insight
to ignite my mind. Where is it?
The walk through the aisles continues.

The Flowers of Spring

All the world is lit by these,
with vibrant shades and hues.
Which one do I like the most?
Oh, so difficult to choose.

Boarded Up

Large, imposing, sturdy...
the picture fastened in my mind
torn in my return to a current reality.
The crispness and vitality of images
in wistful memory dissipated
by convergence with present day dinge.
Essence of neighborhood vibrancy
shuttered by boarded up windows...
windows that once allowed light into my life.

Now missing, those sounds that filled
this shell of a once living structure...
my mother's laughter...
my father's songs that resounded
each day...
Galway Bay...The Foggy Dew...The Black Velvet Band...
verses that became imbedded...that connected his
youth with mine.
I search for the well of my being.
I look beyond the Newark neighborhood.

They gather around the fireplace in Glenavoo.
Music pours from the small house of rough stone...
stone hewn by the ages.
A young boy sits with rapt attention,
embraced by the music.
People with little beyond
a poverty existence, buoyed only by
the tunes that surround in the
birthplace of my father's song.

I hear the sounds of those verses rippling
across Lough Talt
and echoing off the green slopes
of the Ox Mountains.
A place of natural beauty...
beauty veiled in poverty...
poverty that drove most away.
I carry the sounds with me in silence.

Lough Talt, County Sligo, bordering the
Glenavoo Deehan homesite

'Tis the Season (Cinquain)

The cards
arrive each day.
Season's Greetings abound.
Merry Christmas...Happy New Year
Peace flows.

Reflection

I look at you and wonder.
What has become of you?
I remember you young and athletic,
filled with optimism, looking forward

to the next chapter,
to the next adventure...new vistas.
So active with your children, now grown,
in distant locations with children of their own.

Now the glint in your eyes missing,
hair graying, shoulders stooped,
with an arthritic knee that will no longer
participate in hiking mountain trails.

No sense of anticipation to start your day.
The wonder gone.
What happened?
I turn and walk away from the mirror.

Winter Haiku

Host trees now discard
spent autumn leaves turned golden,
pine for Winter's sleep.

Winter solstice here.
Darkness sends shadow too soon.
Long night's sleep ahead.

Icicles dangle.
Winter's white wrath now surrounds.
Wood fires will crackle.

White wreaths cling to doors.
Snow lays its heavy blanket.
Shovels dance gay jigs.

Bright star lights manger
and also Santa's skyway.
Amazon claims night.

PART 4

PROSE FICTION

Lost Ball

Sitting in his chair, Bill Jackson lowered the book and let it rest in his lap. He closed his eyes and felt the luxurious drowsiness that comes with an afternoon nap. Pleasant memories of bygone days filtered through his mind as he drifted into twilight.

His peaceful somnolence was suddenly shattered by the piercing yells of children. He rose from his chair and walked to the window with the groggy hangover effect of an unfulfilled nap. The noise was coming from the Crowthers' spacious backyard next door. Looking over the five-foot wooden fence, he saw Tommy and several of his friends playing whiffle ball. His annoyance level began to rise. How many times had a much-sought afternoon nap been ruined by these neighborhood noisemakers.

He watched the ten-year-olds play for a few minutes. Every time a batter would strike the ball solidly, one group of the boys would yell excitedly to support his run around the bases, while a fielder scampered to retrieve it and throw hurriedly back to an infielder. Their enthusiasm for the ballgame was real. Each batter tried his best to smash the ball and the fielders dutifully ran down each ball hit into the field of play.

Jackson went back to his chair and read the newspaper for a few minutes. Then he grabbed the remote control and turned on the five o'clock local news. It was a good way to offset the noise of the play next door. After several minutes the doorbell sounded and he went to answer the door. He opened it and there stood Tommy Crowther wearing his Braves baseball cap.

"Hi Mr. Jackson. Billy Foley hit my whiffle ball into your yard. Would you please see if you can find it for me?"

Jackson stood there annoyed for a moment not quite sure what had happened or what to say. Without giving it much thought he blurted, "I'm busy right now. I'll look tomorrow."

"Oh––okay. You could just toss it back over the fence."

"I said I'll look tomorrow."

Tommy lowered his head, turned and walked away.

Jackson went back to his chair and resumed watching the local news report.

When the news ended at six o'clock, he went out to the kitchen to prepare dinner. He was torn between microwaving the Stouffer's frozen lasagna dinner or heating a can of Campbell's Italian Wedding soup. He decided on the lasagna. He opened the carton, placed the frozen dinner in the microwave and started it with the timer set for seven minutes.

He thought back to the days when he enjoyed cooking. He tried to do creative meals for Carol periodically. She liked most of the dishes he prepared. His cassoulet was her favorite. Now, cooking seemed mechanical and laborious. Creativity in the kitchen meant nothing. For who would be there to praise it?

He looked out the window into the backyard, then opened the door leading to the yard and walked out. There was no one in the Crowther yard. He looked around his yard and saw no sign of a ball. Assuming one of the boys had scaled the fence and retrieved it, he began to anger. He had a clear understanding with his neighbors––no children were allowed to climb over the fence. He had explained his concern about a child falling and getting injured. In reality, his deeper concern was the possibility of the children damaging one of his plants or scuffing his fence.

He moved carefully around the perimeter of the yard inspecting the areas near the plantings. He spotted a flash of white through the branches of a Hawthorne bush. Bending down, he reached between the branches and pulled out the whiffle ball. It was heavily scuffed and nicked. He looked at it for a moment, then walked to the trash container at the side of his house and tossed it in. He walked back into his kitchen and opened a bottle of Heineken. A minute later the microwave beeper sounded. He retrieved the once frozen entrée from the microwave and proceeded to eat his dinner.

Upon finishing the meal, he took a second beer from the refrigerator and went back to his favorite chair in the living room. He spent the next three hours watching various television shows he was not especially interested in. He then retired to his bed for the night.

The following morning Jackson slept late, not waking until 8:30. After his normal bathroom routine, he dressed and then prepared his regular breakfast––Kellogg's Corn Flakes with sliced banana and milk. He watched the local television news show to get a report on the expected weather for that day. He still didn't believe in checking the internet for such information.

It was a sunny, warm morning and was expected to remain that way. There was no sound of the children at play. Normally they were already outside by this time. Was that because they didn't have a ball?

He began to reflect on what he had done the previous evening.

He thought his anger was justified because of his nap being interrupted. Why did they have to be so loud? Jackson thought back to whiffle ball games from decades ago. He didn't recall ever disturbing anyone in his childhood city neighborhood. Perhaps the neighborhood adults were bothered, but just never expressed their annoyance. His eyes welled with those memories. He began to have some second thoughts.

He walked out to the side of his house and lifted the plastic lid of the trash container. It was empty. The trash collectors had already been there early that morning.

He went back into the house. After a few minutes he retrieved his car keys hanging near the garage door, got in his car and drove ten minutes to the Walmart at the edge of town.

Jackson walked into the very large Walmart. He was only familiar with locations of items he normally shopped for. He looked for an employee to whom he could ask for the location of Sports and Toys sections. Not surprisingly, no employee was to be found.

After wandering the aisles for a few minutes, he located the Sports section. He walked up one aisle without success but in the second aisle he found what he was looking for. On a shelf were whiffle balls inserted in cardboard with plastic overlay packaging. Next to that display he noticed whiffle ball bats with balls packaged in similar cardboard and plastic.

He stood there for a moment looking at both displays. He put the ball he had picked up back on the shelf and then selected the bat and ball combination. Having decided on his selection, he walked to the register area to pay for his purchase.

Jackson arrived home shortly after noon and decided to have some lunch. In accord with his normal routine, he prepared a ham and cheddar cheese sandwich.

After that he retrieved the whiffle ball and bat and walked next door to the Crowther house. He rang the doorbell, waited for a few moments, then rang it again. No one answered.

He started to walk home and saw Margie Stoneham, a nearby neighbor, working in her front garden. She yelled to him, "Hi, Bill. Are you going to play ball to day?"

"No," he replied with a smile. "I'm just dropping off something for Tommy."

"Oh. I saw the Crowthers leave about fifteen minutes ago. Karen said they were going to see her mother today."

"Okay. Thanks. Have a nice day."

"You too."

Jackson went back to his house and dropped off the ball and bat. He decided to drive over to the golf club and hit some balls at the range. Maybe he could pick up a game that afternoon. He would take care of his delivery to Tommy tomorrow.

The following day he had several errands to run in the morning. He had the oil changed in his car, followed by stops at the Post Office, the dry cleaner, and the Publix grocery. He then decided to have a sandwich at the local deli, his favorite lunch spot. They made a great Reuben.

After returning home he put the groceries and dry cleaning away. He placed the whiffle ball and bat in a closet and sat down to watch the Colonial Classic Golf Tournament for a while. He became engrossed in what was a close battle between Jordan Spieth and Sergio Garcia for the lead. After watching them play for a few holes, he started to become a little drowsy. In a couple of minutes, he dozed off in the chair. It was the customary time for his nap.

After a few minutes had passed, he was startled awake by loud yells. Not sure at first as to what it was, it took a few moments to understand he was being woken by the children who were playing next door. As usual, he was quite annoyed by the disruption of his nap.

He arose from his chair and walked to the window. Tommy Crowther was playing in the yard next door with his friends. Instead of whiffle ball, they were playing a game of two-hand touch football. Running about the yard, the boys appeared to be their usual energetic selves.

Jackson stood and thought for a few minutes. Should he take the ball and bat to Tommy now or should he wait and bring it to the Crowther house later after Tommy's friends were gone? He decided there was no time like the present.

After retrieving the ball and bat from the closet, he went out the front door and crossed over to the walkway that ran alongside of the Crowthers' house. He walked to the gate entrance to the backyard. The boys were so engrossed in their football game they didn't notice him standing there.

Jackson called out, "Hello Tommy."

The boys stopped play. Tommy said, "Oh, hi, Mr. Jackson."

"Tommy, I have something for you. I accidentally ran over your ball with my lawn mower a couple of days ago. I went out and bought you a new ball, along with a bat. So take it and have some fun with your friends." Tommy had a quizzical look on his face, but replied, "Okay, thanks Mr. Jackson."

"You're very welcome, Tommy."

Tommy took the ball and bat and placed them at the side of his house.

He immediately ran to rejoin his friends. They resumed their football game.

Jackson returned to his house with a sense of satisfaction. The golf match was still on the television. He sat down and watched the ongoing competition. Periodic yells continued to erupt from next door.

A little while later, he decided to check on the play next door. He walked to a window and peered at the Crowther's backyard. The boys continued to run plays in their game of two-hand touch. The packaged ball and bat still rested at the side of the house. Based on the sounds he heard for the rest of the afternoon, he knew that whiffle ball had not yet reentered the boys' lives.

Over the next few days life continued much the same. Jackson had some doctors' appointments and household chores to attend to, as well as a morning golf match one day. His quotidian habits included his afternoon nap, and on most days slumber was interrupted by the playful yells from next door. With every such occurrence, he would look to the yard next door and see Tommy and his friends playing football. The whiffle ball and bat still rested at the side of the Crowther house in their original packaging.

On Thursday of that week, it rained throughout most of the day. That afternoon he watched golf on television. The golf tournament was being played in the sunshine of South Florida. He dozed off while watching the tournament. There was no interruption to his nap that day. After twenty minutes he awoke naturally and felt refreshed.

He looked out the window facing the Crowther house. There was no play on this rainy day. The ball and bat lay still in the steady rain, the cardboard edge at the top of the packaging now limped with its soggy weight. It seemed the sagging package was staring back at him with a forlorn look.

Jackson ate his microwave heated dinner that night pondering what he had done and the reaction to it. Varied feelings rolled through is mind— rejection, anger, sadness, acceptance. His mood changed from moment to moment. He tried to remember how he thought of things as a boy. It was long ago. He realized he had no idea how he thought as a boy.

Friday was a sunny warm day. He peered out the window. The ball and bat with its sorrowful look still stood there. Jackson went about his chores. That afternoon there was another football game in the Crowther yard. It of course interrupted his nap.

Late that afternoon Jackson looked out at the Crowther yard. The boys' football game was over. No one was in the yard. Jackson walked out his front door and, as stealthily as he could, proceeded alongside the Crowther house. He quietly opened the gate to the yard and went to pick up the still damp ball and bat package.

Jackson quietly walked back to the front of his house and turned onto the walkway that ran alongside it. He went to the trashcan, lifted its cover and dropped in the wilted act of repentance.

He returned to his kitchen and heated a can of Campbell's Chicken Noodle Soup. Sipping from a newly opened Heineken, he decided he would call the golf club in the morning and ask to be slotted into the tee time of a group that didn't have a full foursome. His regular foursome buddies weren't available. Dick Creighton and Larry Wallace were out of town visiting family and Chip Bailey would be at the Boys and Girls Club doing his weekly volunteer work.

After a few weeks went by, Jackson let the matter disappear from his mind. The whiffle ball anger had dissolved and he was into a new routine. He moved the site of his afternoon reading and ensuing nap into a spare bedroom where he had another comfortable sitting chair. It was a part of the house most distant from the Crowther backyard. With no noise to disturb him, he could enjoy his nap without interruption.

As the calendar marched into December, his visits to the golf course declined. His normal cutoff for playing golf was 50 degrees Fahrenheit and most days now failed to achieve that benchmark. Less golf also meant less interaction with his golfing buddies.

That was the part of golf outings he missed the most. The banter and kibitzing with the guys, he realized, was more important than the golf shots. Indeed, the latter, more often than not, left him frustrated when he departed from the golf course.

In addition, with Christmas now approaching, he felt a cloud of depression setting in. Being a widower now with his children living several hundred miles away created the prospect of a lonely Christmas. The foreshadowing made him sure to have a supply of engrossing books to carry him through the season into the New Year. Based on a couple of books he was now reading, he felt he had met that goal.

Three days before Christmas, Jackson sat in his new reading chair. After having completed some errands that morning and finishing a light lunch, he wanted to get back into a novel he had gotten from the library.

A few minutes after he had begun reading, he heard the doorbell ring. He opened the door and saw Karen Crowther and Tommy standing before him.

"Hello Bill," said Karen.

"Hi Karen. Hi Tommy."

"Hi Mr. Jackson."

"What a surprise. What brings you two here?"

"Tommy, why don't you tell Mr. Jackson why we are here."

"Okay Mom. Well, hmm. I guess I wanna give you these golf balls 'cause you were nice to me."

Tommy handed a sleeve of new Titleist golf balls to Jackson.

Jackson looked at the golf balls and, as a shadow of guilt started to encroach, said, "Wow, Tommy, this is awfully nice of you. I don't remember doing anything to deserve such a nice present."

"Tommy, remind Mr. Jackson how he was nice to you."

"Well, you bought me a whiffle ball and bat. But I don't know where they are."

"Tommy, you shouldn't have mentioned that."

"I'm sorry Mom. I forgot not to say that."

"Well, Bill, I'm afraid Tommy did misplace them and couldn't remember where he left them. He thought he had left them outside the house but we could never find them. He must have left them somewhere else. He felt so bad about losing them after you had bought them for him."

"Oh," said Bill as his face started to redden. "I'm sorry to hear that."

"Well, that's behind us now," said Karen.

"I'm sorry I didn't take care of it better, Mr. Jackson."

"Oh, that's okay, Tommy."

"Bill, we hope you have a nice Christmas."

The Crowthers departed and Bill went back to his chair. He couldn't get back into reading. Guilt now fully enveloped him. He argued with himself as to whether the guilt was deserved or not. In the end he couldn't sustain his rationalization of innocence.

The next morning Jackson got into his car and drove to Walmart. What he was looking for was out of season and he didn't think his trip would be successful. He searched the sporting goods section for several minutes without success. Finally, he found an employee and inquired as to whether they had any whiffle ball and bat sets. The employee said that item was out of season but would look to see if any items might still remain. Sure enough, the employee found a set in an obscure place. Jackson made the purchase and, with some relief, headed home.

The following day was Christmas Eve. Around noon, Jackson walked over to the Crowther's house with the wiffle ball package under his arm and rang the doorbell. Steve Crowther answered the door.

"Hello Bill."

"Hi Steve. The other day Karen and Tommy told me that the wiffle ball set I got him a couple of months ago had somehow been lost. I didn't want him to go through Christmas with that on his mind so I decided to get him a replacement."

Jackson handed the wiffle ball package to Crowther.

"Bill, you didn't have to do that. It wasn't your fault Tommy lost it." Jackson felt the guilt regenerating in his mind and sheepishly said, "Oh, I just didn't want Tommy worrying about it."

"You're so nice to do that. Tommy is out with Karen and Julie at the moment, but I'll be sure to give it to him as soon as they get home."

"That's great, Steve. Have a Merry Christmas."

"You have a Merry Christmas too, Bill." Jackson turned and started to walk away.

"Say, Bill. I know you're by yourself now. Why don't you come over and join us for dinner on Christmas?"

"Oh no, but thank you. I don't want to get in the way."

"You won't be in the way. It's just the four of us. Adding a fifth spot at the table is no big deal. I insist you join us."

Jackson thought for a moment and gave in. "Well alright, but don't do anything special for me."

"It will be special just to have you with us. Come over around three o'clock."

"Well, okay. I'll see you then."

Jackson went home and sat in his chair. He picked up his book but didn't open it. He reflected on all that had taken place. His mind took him back to the beginning. He was the one who had thrown away the original whiffle ball and then lied about accidentally destroying it with a lawn mower. He was the one who picked up and threw away the replacement ball and bat in a package. Tommy felt guilty thinking he had somehow lost it. Jackson knew that it was he who should be steeped in guilt. Now the family is going out of its way to be nice to him on Christmas Day.

The following morning as Jackson sat eating his Cornflakes, he decided he would own up that afternoon to his guilt. He would let the Crowther family know that he had thrown away the original whiffle ball, as well as the replacement whiffle ball set.

At 3:00pm Jackson walked across his front yard to the Crowther's house and rang the front door bell. Steve welcomed him in and they proceeded to the den. Jackson accepted the offer of a beer and they proceeded to watch the Lakers–Celtics game on TV. Jackson wasn't an especially big fan of basketball but he enjoyed the aspect of watching a sporting event with another person. It was something he had not been able to do in quite some time.

While they watched the game, Karen was in the kitchen preparing the dinner with sporadic help from Julie, the Crowther's teenage daughter. Tommy was engrossed in Legos construction in the living room, a good part of which was occupied by a fully decorated Christmas tree and various boxes and wrapping paper scattered about.

Jackson ducked into the kitchen for a moment just when Karen was moving a golden-brown turkey from a roasting pan to a large dish. Julie was sitting at the kitchen table with her eyes fixed on the cell phone in her hand.

"Hello Karen. That's a beautiful looking bird you have there."

"Hi Bill. We're so glad you could join us today."

"Thank you for inviting me. It's very nice of all of you to be sharing part of your Christmas with me."

"Oh, don't mention it. Julie, please go tell your father that it's time to carve the turkey."

Without taking her eyes from her phone Julie got up from her chair and walked out of the kitchen expressionless.

About twenty minutes later everyone was seated at a dining room table and began to eat the Christmas dinner. Steve and Karen were seated at each end while Jackson was on a side facing Tommy and Julie.

After a few minutes of pleasantries, Jackson said, "Well Tommy, was Santa Claus good to you?"

Julie looked up with a somewhat disdainful expression as though she had just heard a stupid question. Tommy, while still in the process of pushing broccoli around his plate, replied, "Yeah, I guess so."

Karen, with a disapproving look, said, "Tommy, tell Mr. Jackson what you got."

"I got a really neat Lego set. I'm building a castle now."

"Is there anything else you can tell him you received?'

Tommy had a puzzled look on his face. After a moment his eyes lit up and he said, "Oh yeah, I got the whiffle ball and bat that you gave me."

"I hope you have some fun with it Tommy."

"I wish I knew what I did with the first set you gave me. I thought it was just outside the house, but I guess not."

"Tommy, I think you should know…"

Julie interjected, "Some creep in the neighborhood probably stole it."

Steve said, "Well, I don't know if that happened but it would be pretty creepy if someone did steal it."

Karen said, "What were you going to say Bill?"

Jackson paused for a moment, feeling an impediment to his planned confession. "Oh nothing, nothing important."

The introduction of a new label that might brand him in the neighborhood had suddenly raised a red flag.

The rest of the dinner proceeded with a new topic. Karen told Jackson about the Crowthers' planned trip to Florida in the coming week. With the children now on Christmas break from school, Steve was taking some vacation time and they would bring in the New Year in Orlando. Tommy was very excited about visiting Disney World. Even Julie dropped her sullen, teenage visage to talk about the coming week.

After dinner Jackson accompanied Steve to watch the start of another basketball game. He stared at the screen but his mind was on the missed opportunity for his confession. At half-time he told Steve he was tired. He excused himself and bade good bye to the Crowther family, thanking them several times for their hospitality.

Jackson went home and sat in his favorite chair. He realized he had squandered his opportunity for confession due to fear of being labeled a neighborhood creep. His guilt would remain an undisclosed part of his being.

The dark brow of winter encircled him. In the dim light Jackson stared at the picture of Carol on the table by his side and thought of their Florida trip seven years ago. He remembered how Disney World had brought out traces of youth from two seventy-year-olds. Now, he never felt any sense of youth. Based on his recent actions, he had actually become hostile to youth.

After pondering for a while, he decided he would call Chip Bailey in the morning. He would ask to accompany him on his next volunteer visit to the Boys and Girls Club and experience what that was like. It would be something new to look forward to.

The Red Convertible

One of the wheels had a notch where a piece of plastic had broken off. I pushed the small grey toy car across the wooden porch floor and felt its uneven roll. Stevie Wilson's sleek little red convertible rolled effortlessly with the slightest forward motion of his hand. How cool was that car! It even sported a slick white stripe along its side and had whitewall tires. Of course, that was one of five or six neat cars that Stevie had. Envy poured through me when I compared my one junky car to his collection.

We played contentedly for a while, pushing cars across the porch in our manufactured chase plots. He would switch his cars for different race adventures, but my grey sedan was called into action for every one. All of his cars looked better than mine, but it was the little red convertible that held my special attention.

At one point Stevie's mother called him into the house for something. In Stevie's absence, I made up my own fantasy scenarios using Stevie's cars. I made believe I was the chaser using the red convertible and, of course, I was successful in catching the other car.

I don't remember consciously making the decision, but at one point I slipped the red convertible into my jacket pocket. When Stevie returned, we continued our fantasy adventures. We played for another half-hour. Stevie never noticed that his red convertible was missing. I was going to ask Stevie if I could borrow the car, but the fear of his learning the car was already in my jacket overtook me. I left him that day with the grey sedan in my hand and the red convertible in my pocket.

* * *

I recounted these events in my mind as Sister Rita Marie took my second-grade class through the preparation for the

Sacrament of Penance in advance of our First Communion. She explained to us the difference between venial and mortal sins. I thought of times when I had disobeyed my mother, including scraping the asparagus off my plate when she wasn't looking, and arguing with my father when he told me to go to bed before The Lone Ranger was over. Also, I had yelled in anger at my friends when games of play didn't go my way. I thought these were venial sins. But then there was the big one––the theft of Stevie Wilson's red convertible toy car. Was this a mortal sin? I wasn't sure, but it had to be close. What other kinds of mortal sins could a seven-year-old commit?

I fretted over this in the days leading up to my first Confession. I really didn't mean anything bad when I took the car. I simply wanted to enjoy playing with it. I couldn't get over the fact though, that I had stolen his car.

On Friday morning Sister Rita led our class across the driveway to Saint Patrick's Church. We walked in boy-girl pairs and were told sternly by her to be quiet and orderly. We sat in pews and were instructed to pray and examine our consciences once more before getting in the confessional lines. The penitent seven-year-olds were called up one row at a time.

When my pew was called, I walked nervously to the front of the Church. I was directed to the line waiting for Fr. O'Neal's confessional. I stood there rehearsing in my mind what I was going to confess. When I thought of my car theft, my knees began to quiver. I didn't know Fr. O'Neal. Was he going to scold and punish me for my crime? I didn't know, but as I inched closer in line, my breathing rate increased. Suddenly next in line, I felt frozen in place.

The door to the Confessional opened and Tony Medillo walked out. He was always in trouble in class. He must have had a bad time with Fr. O'Neal, although he still had the normal cocky smirk on his face. Maybe Fr. O'Neal wasn't too bad after all.

In I walked and knelt in the semi-darkness. I was aware of my breathing again. Fr. O'Neal slid open a wooden slat and there was a screen between us. The presence of the screen made me feel a little safer.

Fr. O'Neal started with a short prayer; and then I nervously spoke, "Forgive me Father for I have sinned. I scraped the asparagus off my plate when Mommy wasn't looking. I argued with Daddy when he wouldn't let me watch The Lone Ranger. I yelled at my friends. But I thought they were cheating me, Father."

Then I stopped.

Fr. O'Neal said, "Is there anything else?"

After pausing with fear that seemed to grip my whole body, I blurted, "I stole Stevie Wilson's car."

"You stole a car?"

"I stole his red convertible toy car––the one with the white stripe and whitewall tires."

I held my breath, awaiting an unknown doom.

"Well, don't do that again. You should never steal, son. Repeat after me the Act of Contrition and for your penance say two Our Fathers and two Hail Marys. Also, give Stevie Wilson his car back."

I walked out of the confessional elated and relieved. My guilt was erased. I was able to breathe normally again. I went back to my pew and read the prayers of penance in my little prayer book.

Later that afternoon I walked slowly from my apartment building down Ninth Street to Stevie Wilson's house. When I was sure that nobody was around, I ran onto the porch and put the little red convertible in front of the door. At that moment the door opened and Stevie stood there.

"Hi Jackie. What are you doing here?"

I froze for a moment. Then in a stammering response, I said, "Uh, hi Stevie. Uh, I guess I'm returning your red convertible."

He looked at me quizzically and said, "Oh, I didn't know you had it."

I stood there in a semi-frozen state for a few moments and then said, "Yeah, I took it 'cause I liked it. Sorry."

Stevie responded, "That's okay. You can play with it anytime."

"Oh, okay. Thanks."

I turned to walk down the steps, as Stevie said, "Heah, do you want to play whiffle ball tomorrow?"

"Sure." I replied. I went down the steps and then ran all the way home.

* * *

That evening my mother served peas with dinner and my father let me watch The Lone Ranger. I had nice dreams in my sleep that night.

Departure

Ireland circa 1950

Michael Cawley stopped his work for a moment of rest and looked out wistfully over the Doocastle field. Peter Kilgoran continued to gather the hay with a large rake as did Michael's younger sister, Kathleen. It was a fine July afternoon and the summer sun felt good on his back. The recent stretch of good weather had dried the cut grass to allow the work to proceed on schedule. He thought another two days like this and they should be finished with his field.

Michael resumed his work and after an hour or so had passed, he called to his sister, "Kat'leen, dat's enough for dis day. Ye go down to da house and tell Maah to prepare da supper. I'll be along shortly."

"Alright Michael. I'll do dat now," she responded.

Kathleen walked over to the cart, picked up her sweater and walked down the narrow boreen toward the house.

Michael turned to Peter and said, "Dat's grand work Peter. Let's finish dis corner of da field and dat will be a good day's labor."

"A good day's labor indeed," replied Peter.

They completed the corner and viewed the section of the large field that was dotted with the reeks they had built that day. Good progress had been made. They speculated they might even finish building the mounds of hay tomorrow. Then they would move on to Peter's field where Michael would reciprocate with assistance to his neighbor.

That evening, Michael, Kathleen and his mother, Brigid, sat at the table over a supper of boiled chicken and potatoes. They talked about news in the village for that was what mattered most to people in this rural part of the country.

Brigid said, "Noreen McGinty is after tellin' me her nephew, Daniel Hanahan, is goin' off to Galway in September to study at da university. He wants to become a barrister.

Declan Kilcoyne, da barrister in Tubbercurry, has told Daniel he can work for him when his schoolin' is done. Ye know Declan is gettin' on in years and he will need da help some day."

Kathleen interjected, "Daniel is a smaert boy. He always had da best grades in class."

Brigid, not hearing, continued, "Sure'n dem barristers makes great money. For wasn't Kilcoyne da first to own a caer in Tubbercurry."

"I'm told dat he was Maah," replied Michael.

Michael's interest lay in the prospect of success in America, not Ireland, and he decided to change the subject. "Peter was tellin' me dis day his brot'er, John, is now in da building trade in Brooklyn and makes great money, probably as great as any barrister in Tubbercurry."

"Don't ye be goin' on about America again," said Brigid. "Ever since our cousin, Martin Flanagan, visited us last summer and filled yer head wit' his fables about America, dat's all ye talk about. It's got murders and gangsters and t'ings ye don't want to be near. Ye know yer place is in Ireland."

"But Maah, ye know dat Michael has always dreamed about America," said Kathleen.

"It's dreamin' enough he does. 'Dere's no time for dreamin' when dere's work to be done on dis faerm."

"Da work gets done on dis faerm Maah, as it always has since I've been runnin' it."

Brigid responded, "It would be a sad day in Ireland if a son was to run off and leave his mot'er and sister to fend for 'demselves."

After they finished eating, Kathleen said, "I'm goin' down to Flaherty's to see Grainee. I should be back in two hours."

Brigid said, "Don't ye be tellin' me it's Grainee ye're goin' to see when I know it's Jimmy ye're really interested in seein'. Eileen Kelly told me she saw ye and young Flaherty walkin' down Teelin' Street yesterday side by side, smilin' and actin' like ye were sweet on one anot'er. I told ye before ye're too young to be interested in a boy who's still figurin' what he's goin' to be doin' wit' his life."

"Oh Maah, I jest happened to see Jimmy on me way to da market and said hello to him. I have to talk to Grainee about her new job at da Cooperative."

After Kathleen left, Brigid and Michael sat at the kitchen table in silence for a while. Michael pondered his cup of tea, then said, "Ye have to face it Maah. Kat'leen is growin' into a young woman and she has new 'tings on her mind."

Brigid replied, "Well she better keep her mind on dis faerm. If ye leave for America, I'll be in a fine state wit' her goin' about wit' her mind in da staers."

The conversation evaporated into silence. After they finished eating, Michael said, "Dat's a lovely supper Maah. I'm goin' to Clancy's fer a pint. I'll be back after a while." Michael put on his coat, walked out the door to his bicycle and pedaled the two miles down the road to the shebeen.

He sat on a wooden stool next to his friend Matt Malloy and said to the barman, "Paddy, a drop of da poteen––and a pint if ye please."

Matt greeted him, "How are ye dis fine evenin' Michael?"

"Aagh, I spent da day gat'erin' da hay wit' Peter and Kat'leen and we finished a good paert of da field. So, it was a satisfyin' day until supper dis evenin'. Me Maah skewered me wit' her tongue when I talked of America. She's a haerd one, she is."

"She's afraid of losin' ye Michael. She fear's da future wit'out you here to keep up da faerm."

"I know dat," replied Michael. "But dere's no need fer her to worry. Kat'leen is finished wit' her schoolin'. She's a strong gerl, and smaert too. She does good work on da faerm. She'll be able to handle da faerm for Maah."

"But Michael, what if she were to marry. I hear dat Kat'leen and Jimmy Flaherty have been spendin' much of deir time toget'er recently."

"Well, ye're right dere Matt. I'm t'inkin' dat she and Jimmy will be gettin' married in a year or two. But here's da t'ing. Jimmy's older brot'er, Liam, has been managin' da Flaherty faerm since deir Paah passed on. Liam's got a wife and two little ones, so he'll not be goin' anywhere. Da faerm is his responsibility now. When Kat'leen and Jimmy get married, dey'll live at our faerm. It would be a sensible move for Jimmy. He'd have da opportunity to manage his own faerm wit' Kat'leen. Maah will have no more worries cloudin' her mind."

"I suppose ye are right," said Matt. "I didn't know about da Flaherty brot'er's situation."

Michael downed his poteen and pondered his own words as he slowly drank the dark porter. He wondered if his forecast of Kathleen and Jimmy's taking over the farm was based on reality or only his hope. He pondered future life in America. Farming wasn't in his blood. He had been managing the farm though, since his older brother, Paddy, died unexpectedly from pneumonia four years earlier. This wasn't the life he wanted. America was his dream. He knew he would soon have to decide on emigration for he couldn't make the move much beyond his current age of twenty-five. To be successful in America a man had to emigrate when he was young.

* * *

The September day was gray with a light rain falling. The weather had been this way for almost two weeks. Michael's days had been occupied with tending to the sheep and the cattle. Kathleen helped with some of the farm work, but on a limited basis. She had recently started working four days a week as a shop girl in Murray's dry goods store in Tubbercurry. Having finished with school, she had no thoughts of going to university. Very few farm girls from Sligo did. Michael now spent most days alone except for the noon meal with his mother.

This day would be different. He walked into the house. His mother was sitting by the fireplace and quietly singing the words of "Galway Bay."

"Maah," said Michael, "Tomorrow I'll be goin' to Ballina. Dere's somet'ing I have to attend to dere and I need to talk to ye about it."

Brigid stopped singing and looked at Michael with fear in her eyes.

"What would ye be goin' to Ballina fer? Dere's no business of da faerm to be done dere."

"I'm goin' to Ballina to see an agent to book passage to America. I plan to leave on a ship out of Cobh in early November. I'll be headed to New York."

Brigid lowered her head and wept. "I feared dis day would come. Oh, how I prayed to God it would not. How can ye do dis? Ye are tearin' me haert. I beg ye son, I beg ye to stay. Kat'leen and I need ye here on da faerm."

"Maah, I know dis is haerd fer ye, but I've told ye many times of me feelin' about America. Me future is dere. I have to do dis."

"No, no, no," she sobbed.

"T'ings will be fine here, Maah. Da worst of da faerm work is done fer dis year. Ye and Kat'leen can take care of da faerm t'rough da winter. In da Spring Peter Kilgoran can help da two of ye wit' da heavier work. Kat'leen can leave her job in Tubbercurry if need be."

Brigid's low sobs continued. "It's not da same. Peter's a good man but he's not paert of dis family. It's just not da same, and Kat'leen likes goin' off to her job each day. She'll not be wantin' to quit dat."

"Well Maah, ye know dat Kat'leen and Jimmy Flaherty have been seein' more and more of each ot'er. One of da reasons she likes da job is dat she gets to see Jimmy most days in Tubbercurry."

"Aagh, don't be goin' on about Jimmy Flaherty. She's sure to...."

Michael interrupted, "Ye've got to face it Maah. Kat'leen has grown into a young woman. Jimmy's da man in her life. Ye're likely to be seein' a marriage in dis family in da future, and it might not be too faer into da future. If dat's da case, Jimmy will be part of da family and he and Kat'leen will be here to run da faerm. Liam Flaherty is managin' da Flaherty faerm, so it's only natural dat Kat'leen and Jimmy would live here at da Cawley faerm."

Brigid replied, "Tis a fairy tale ye are spinnin'––nut'in' more than a fairy tale."

"It's not da fairies makin' up a tale Maah. Ye'll find out soon enough."

Michael was about to say something else but hesitated. He looked at his mother for a moment and said, "I'll be checkin' on da cows. I'll be back after a while."

Brigid stared blankly at the glowing bars in the fireplace for a brief time. She lowered her head to her hands. Her quiet sobs grew into a wailing.

* * *

On an early October evening Michael walked into Clancy's shebeen and, seeing Liam Flaherty, sat next to him at the bar.

"I haven't seen much of ye in da last little while Liam. How have ye been gettin' on?"

Liam replied, "I'm well Michael. Between work on da faerm and helpin' me wife wit da wee ones, I've not been gettin'out much to see people."

"Aagh, I understand. I understand indeed."

"I'm hearin' from me sister, Grainee, dat ye are soon headin' for America. Is dat right, Michael?"

"Indeed I am, Liam. T'ree weeks from dis day I leave on a train for Cork and da next day I'm on a ship sailin' da Atlantic fer New York."

"Well, dat's a grand t'ing fer ye Michael. Ye'll be findin' gold on da streets of New York," chuckled Liam. "Dat's what dey say. But sure, ye'll be missed in dese parts, especially by yer Maah and Kat'leen. How do ye t'ink dey will get on wit'out ye?"

"It's good ye bring dat point up Liam. I've been wantin' to talk wit' ye on dat matter."

"Oh, have ye?"

"Ye know dat yer brother Jimmy and me sister Kat'leen have been seein' a lot of each ot'er, actin' like love birds. Dey kept it quiet for a while, but now deir romance is well known. From somet'ings dat Kat'leen has said to me, I'm inferrin' dat da two of dem will be marryin'––and sooner rather dan later."

Liam replied, "I've been gettin' a sense of dat meself. I know Jimmy's over da moon wit' Kat'leen. It wouldn't surprise me if he'd be proposin' to her soon."

"Well," said Michael, "da way I see it, if Jimmy and Kat'leen were to get married next year, dey will live in our house. Wit' me gone, der's plenty of room fer dem and me Maah. Da two of dem will run da faerm and can watch after Maah. I know dat da Flaherty faerm is yer's to manage now, so it would be a perfect set up fer Jimmy to help take over da Cawley faerm."

"I understand what ye're sayin' Michael. Jimmy's a good lad and a good worker. I've never gotten da sense dough dat Jimmy likes da faermin' work. His mind is always caught up in da t'ings he sees at da cinema—cowboys and adventures and faer away places and such. But I t'ink if da Cawley faerm were his responsibility he would be focused on da faermin' and put his heart into it. He wouldn't be t'inkin' about dose flighty tings dat young lads dwell on. It would be a grand opportunity fer Jimmy––and Kat'leen."

* * *

Early on a Tuesday morning Kathleen sat with her mother at the kitchen table eating breakfast. No one spoke. Finally Brigid broke the silence.

"In six more days Michael will be leavin'. I'll never see me son again. He'll be as dead to me as his poor brot'er, Paddy. Da two of us will be havin' a wake that day. I still can't believe me son is leavin' me."

Kathleen, with her eyes down, said quietly, "Ye will get t'rough dis Maah."

"At least I will still have me daughter by me side. Dat is me only comfort."

Kathleen said nothing and quietly sipped her tea. The silence hung heavily in the room and lasted for a few minutes until Kathleen spoke.

"Maah, I have to leave early today. Mr. Murray needs me to put away some of the new stock."

With that she got up and went over to her mother at the sink. She thought her mother looked older and frailer than the image of her she kept in her mind. Kathleen embraced her mother in a long-lasting hug and said, "I love ye dearly Maah."

Brigid felt slightly ill at ease for that was a type of affection not normally shown by Kathleen. She thought it was due to Michael's impending departure for America.

"Ye're a fine daughter," said Brigid in response.

Kathleen quietly turned and walked out the door.

Brigid cleared the dishes from the table. She then walked to the window by the door and watched Kathleen as she rode her bicycle down the boreen until she disappeared over the rise.

Later that afternoon Michael was tending to a limping cow on one of the farm's distant fields. His mind was more on his upcoming move to America than on the cow. He saw it as the opening of a new world of opportunity for him. Ever since his cousin, Martin, visited the family last year and spoke of the wonders of that land across the sea, he was determined to make the move. His dream was soon to become reality.

Despite the excitement he also felt a deepening sense of guilt about leaving his mother. To leave her as an elderly woman on this farm was nothing for a son to be proud of. He rationalized and overcame this internal conflict with his now certain thinking that Kathleen would marry Jimmy Flaherty and the two of them would run the farm and properly look after his mother. This scenario helped to assuage his guilt.

Michael looked up from the cow and saw Peter Kilgoran running toward him and yelling. "Michael, come quickly. Yer mot'er's in a bad way. Come quickly."

Michael dropped the bag of feed. Peter continued, "Ye have to come quickly Michael. Noreen McGinty was payin' a visit to yer house and found yer motter layin' on the floor. She was awake but not respondin' to Noreen. Noreen ran to our house to tell me. I went over and found yer mot'er in the same state. Me wife went down the road to the post office and placed a telephone call to Doctor Corcoran. He was jest arrivin' at the house when I left. I'm sorry it took me a while to get here Michael. I didn't know where ye were."

Michael immediately began to run across the field to the boreen that led to the house. The distance seemed interminable. As he got closer, he saw Dr. Corcoran, with the help of Noreen, placing his mother in the back seat of his car.

* * *

The next morning the volunteer driver from Sligo General Hospital dropped Michael off at his house. His mother had had a stroke. The doctor said that her condition was stable and she should survive. She was completely paralyzed on her left side but was conscious and alert. She had been desperately trying to tell Michael something but her speech was garbled and he couldn't understand her words. There was look of alarm in her eyes. Michael had not seen Kathleen and had not been able to get in touch with her. From the hospital he had placed a phone call to Murray's but Mr. Murray, in an agitated state, said she had not shown up for work yesterday and didn't know where she was.

Michael decided he would ride his bicycle to Flaherty's to see if she was there or if anyone knew her whereabouts. First, he would get some bedclothes together for his mother to take back to the hospital. He walked into Brigid's room and, on her bed, saw a piece of paper which he picked up.

26 October

Dear Mother,
I write to ye this day to let ye know that I will be gone for what I hope will not be a long absence. I'm letting ye know about something which ye may already suspect. Jimmy Flaherty and I have fallen in love, and I have accepted his proposal of marriage. This is a wonderful thing for the two of us.
Another wonderful thing has happened, although you may not see it that way. Jimmy has secured a job in the brick-laying trade in Liverpool. This position was promised to him in a letter from his friend, Bernie Sullivan. Bernie said the job was his if he could be in Liverpool before the end of October. Bernie has been working as a bricklayer in Liverpool for the last two years. Jimmy and I have left for Dublin and will be traveling by boat to Liverpool on 27 October.
I know this is troubling news for ye and I am sorry for that. This is a good thing for Jimmy and me. I have to do it. I'm sure once we are settled, we will be able to make visits back to Ireland and see ye.
I will write to ye soon with more information.

Your loving daughter,
Kathleen

In a daze Michael walked into the kitchen and sat at the table. He reread the letter very slowly, hoping he had terribly misread it the first time.

He stared at the peat ashes in the fireplace for some time. Michael finally turned away and picked up the packet that contained his travel documents. He knew by heart what they said, but wanted to read them again.

> *S.S. Marine Jumper*
> *Departure – Cobh, County Cork, Ireland*
> *November 2, 1950 11:00am*
> *Room No. A22, Berth 7*
> *Arrival – New York, New York, USA*
> *November 7, 1950*

Michael took a deep breath. He got up and dropped the papers in the ash pail by the fireplace. He went out the door to his bicycle and began to pedal down the boreen with the hope that Clancy's shebeen would be open and with the certainty he would stay until it closed.

Windfall

Sam never expected it to turn out this way. His dreams were all he could foresee. He had thought of the things he would be able to do, the perceived freedoms that would enhance his life, the joys that would fill it.

Just a weekly habit. In reality that's all he thought it would ever be, despite his dreams. Typically, it would be right after he filled his pickup truck on Friday—two packs of Marlboro, two six packs of Bud Light for the weekend, and two Mega Millions Lottery tickets. Then the first stop at Maguire's to knock back a couple with the guys. Usually with the same trio: Robbie, Bill and Mike. It was a chance to swap stories and have a few laughs, with the intended limit of two rounds. Now and then it would stretch beyond and he would encounter Kathy's wrath over missing dinner with her and the two children. He would try to bear the tirade without response but occasionally he would unleash vitriol with regret to follow. On those evenings, the end result would be his disappointment with the father image he left with his children.

He would always attempt to correct course for the rest of the weekend with fatherly focus on the kids' activities— little league, soccer, gymnastics, plus church on Sunday—all the things Peggy had choreographed for the family.

The normal workweek would resume on Monday. A Tuesday evening ritual would be tuning in for the drawing of the Lottery numbers. Of course, his combination never appeared on the screen. Life went on in this manner week after week, and year after year.

On one particular Tuesday evening, he sat in front of the television with tickets in hand. The Lottery prize had grown to $165,000,000. He waited for the numbers to appear on the screen, with his usual high hope and minimal expectation.

06-84-23-35

The first four drawn numbers matched one of his tickets. His heart rate suddenly increased.

    32

He looked at his ticket…looked at the screen. The fifth number matched. He stopped breathing. He knew what the last number on his ticket was.

    67!

His body started shaking. He tried to call Kathy but no words would come out. His scream could be heard throughout the neighborhood.

* * *

Four years later after the echoes of that shriek have long subsided, Sam sits on his spacious deck looking past the palmettos toward the breaking waves. It is a sunny, pleasant late afternoon. Only a scattering of people is on this section of the Hilton Head Island beach, fronted by large, imposing homes, and comfortably distant from the hotels and crowds he takes pain to avoid. He now allows a few select people into his current life.

Kathy had left with the children eighteen months earlier. She wanted no more of the high-end, big ticket lifestyle Sam had adopted for the family. His obsessions with grand toys––the Viking 82 Skybridge yacht, the Mazzerattis, the leased Embraer jet––were in her opinion giving the children a twisted view of the world, one they couldn't comprehend. The more extravagances in which Sam indulged, the more Kathy wanted her idea of normal life. They grew apart. Sam extolled their opportunity that few people had. She viewed it as a curse rather than an opportunity.

Kathy took the children and her share of the fortune, and moved into an upper middle-class neighborhood with tree lined streets. It belied her degree of wealth but allowed some sense of normalcy in their lives despite the separation from Sam.

As Sam sips Grey Goose on his beachfront deck, he thinks back to the days of camaraderie with his pals at Maguire's and the enjoyment of the bantering and kibitzing. His intent after winning the fortune was to continue his weekly get-together with Robbie, Bill and Mike. They had welcomed him as their celebrity friend. He of course now paid for their drinks, as well as the drinks for the entire bar crowd.

This pattern continued at Maguire's for a number of weeks. After leaving the bar one Friday evening, he reflected on the evening and concluded that his experience there was no longer the same as it used to be. Sure, his pals were still there and most of the crowd was the same. He realized though, his act of buying drinks for all was not viewed as an act of generosity––just his obligation. He also realized that he was no longer viewed as one of them. He stopped going to Maguire's.

Another change, one that he saw almost immediately, was that many outsiders wanted a piece of him. Investment specialists, insurance hawkers, lawyers, business schemers, venture dreamers, countless charities, and more.

Sam had no idea how to manage wealth. Coupled with his naïveté and generally trusting nature, he had several disastrous encounters with miscreants who were successful in getting their claws into his fortune. Over time, after he saw some of his millions disappear, he realized the larcenous intent of the many people who sought to *help him*. He was fortunate to eventually establish contact with a trustworthy financial advisor who offered sound advice and shielded him from the leeches. The barrier between him and the outside world was firmly planted.

At this point, aside from his children and a very few select others, his financial advisor is a person with whom he has ongoing contact. He is now wary of people and isolated. He doesn't enjoy his toys as much, in part because he has no friends to share them with. Even the jet getaway to his

Caribbean hideaway has lost its luster. He is basically fearful of establishing meaningful contact with people. His Hilton Head deck is the only place where he feels comfortable. Comfort comes with his increasing isolation.

As he sips another Grey Goose, Sam gazes out at the fading daylight. The beach is now devoid of people. The minutes turn to hours.

He tries to remember how happy he was with Kathy when it was just the two of them starting their marriage adventure. He recalls the laughter and love they shared in raising their children. Prior to his lottery win, Kathy was the one who held them together as a cohesive family with love and purpose. He realizes that she was right about what was really important and that he still holds her in his heart.

The darkness of the sky now blends with the darkness of the sea. No line of demarcation separates them. Just one large black wall before his eyes.

He pours another Grey Goose and notes the bottle is now empty. He wonders about his future but sees only emptiness there.

The next morning Sam awakes in a groggy state with a headache. Following a light breakfast and two cups of coffee, his mind begins to clear. He knows what he must do.

He calls Kathy and tells her he has rethought things about his life and acknowledges that she was right in her views on material aspects of their new wealth. He says he wants to become a more positive influence on the children's lives. He asks if she would be willing to have lunch with him that week so that he could discuss his thoughts in more detail. After expressing some initial reluctance, Kathy finally agrees to a lunch meeting.

Sam ends the call with a sense of relief. He doesn't know where the lunch with Kathy will lead, but is confident it is a positive step and hopes new direction in his life will ensue. For the first time since they separated, he feels good about himself.

Sam walks out onto his deck and stares for several moments at the blue ocean, sparkling in the morning sunlight. He picks up the empty Grey Goose bottle and throws it in the trash.

Genesis

He stands motionless in front of me, his eyes dark and without expression. I can't tell whether he holds me in contempt or if he has no feeling for me at all. Memories race through my mind at 100 mph. I sit here frozen, except for the shaking of my knees. Fear of the present, regrets about the past. Only the fear traps tears inside.

* * *

"Please Anthony. You have to stay in school. You get good grades and you only have one year until you graduate."

"No Ma. I'm tired of school. I gotta chance to work for Mr. Cardone and make some money. I'm gonna quit school."

"But Sister Josita says you're a smart boy. You could go to Rutgers like your brother and get a college education. You could make a good life for yourself, Anthony."

"Ma, Johnny's goin' to Rutgers 'cause he got money for fightin' da Krauts. We don't have any money. How could I go to Rutgers? Besides I can help you out with somma what I make. Vinnie's been workin' for Mr. Cardone for six months and he makes good money."

"What kind of business does Mr. Cardone have?"

"He's in da shippin' business, Ma. I'd be makin' deliveries and pickups in da Central Ward. His business is growin' and he needs more help...and da work won't be dat hard."

"I don't know Anthony. This doesn't sound right. I want you to stay in school."

"School's over, Ma!"

That's how the conversation with Ma went. Four days later I walked into Louie Mosconi's newspaper and candy store on Central Avenue. He looked at me nervously.

"Louie, I was here with Vinnie last week to warn you. You still owe Frank fifty bucks. You gotta stay current with your book and you ain't current. It's time to pay up...now."

"I just paid for my candy delivery this morning, Anthony. I don't have the cash. Just give me two more days. The business will give me enough to cover it. I'll pay then. I swear."

I remember like yesterday the fear in Louie's eyes when I moved toward him. I smashed him in the face and he fell down against the comics' shelves, blood pouring from his nose and onto a Superman cover. He looked dazed, so small and helpless, but I didn't care. I took $27.42 from the register and left. That number stays stuck in my mind. The sense of power from my first solo job was thrilling. Oh, how I wanted to feel that again. And I often did. There were plenty of jobs from Frank Cardone over the years, many of them more brutal and even deadly, but the high I got from the first one topped them all.

A few days after that encounter with Louie Mosconi I bought Ma some roses. She thanked me, but I didn't see any happiness in her face. Her eyes filled with tears.

* * *

He walks back toward me. My knees still shake but I can't move. My legs and arms are strapped to the chair. He attaches electrodes to various parts of my body and then his hand moves toward me with a blindfold. Everything turns black. I see Ma's face with tears flowing down her cheeks. I start to sob.

Help Wanted!

I walk to the front of the room and place my papers on the lectern, having handed a copy to Professor Judith. I always look forward to reciting my writing efforts in this OLLI class. Often, I get valuable feedback from my fellow writers and from Professor Judith.

A knock on the door catches me off guard. An OLLI staff person enters the room and apologizes for the interruption. She asks if there is a doctor in the room or someone with a medical background. Apparently, there has been an incident somewhere in the OLLI building. A fellow writing classmate, who is a doctor, rises and follows the woman to wherever the incident has occurred.

At that point I gather myself and go on to read my work, hoping to impress with the words I deliver. Frankly though, it doesn't seem that important now in light of the difficulty someone in the building may be having.

After finishing my presentation and returning to my seat, I think to myself that this situation is similar to some other ones in my life. One time on a trans-Atlantic flight, a passenger had collapsed in a lavatory. Following an intercom call for medical help, a doctor soon made his way forward to render assistance. I later found out that the stricken passenger had in fact recovered. He apparently had had an adverse reaction to some medication. With the doctor's care and consultation, the passenger was soon back in his seat resting comfortably.

There have been a couple of other instances in my life in which an unexpected medical emergency of some type has occurred soon followed by the ubiquitous query seen on film and stage of "Is there a doctor in the house?" In each of these type instances I'm left with a certain sense of inadequacy. Being in a setting where a person may be in dire straits, I would like to have the ability, and the responsiveness, to help. Not demonstrating that ability does make me feel somewhat of a non-contributor to societal crisis situations.

As I ponder this, my mind wanders....

I hear a knock on the classroom door. An OLLI staff person enters with an expression of concern and asks, "Is there an accountant in the room?"

Immediately, I rise from my chair and state, "I'm a CPA. How can I help?"

"We have a distraught student in another room. I think she needs immediate attention. Please follow me."

I follow down the hall and we enter a small conference room. There sits a woman with a checkbook, bank statements, cancelled checks and various papers strewn across the table. She is agitated and mumbles oaths under her breath.

With a bit of hesitation I say, "Excuse me, you seem to be having some trouble."

She casts a look of bewilderment my way and says with a tone of frustration, "Oh, I'm so lost. I'm trying to see if my check book balance is right and the more I look at the bank statements and checks, the more lost I become."

"Oh, I see. Why did you come to the OLLI building to do this?"

"It was so noisy at my daughter's house with the kids playing and laughing, I couldn't concentrate. I thought finding a quiet, empty room at OLLI would help me, but it hasn't."

She crumples some hand written papers and pushes them aside. She looks blankly at the table and emits a long sigh.

"Well, my name is Joe. I'm an OLLI student and I have some background in financial matters. Would it be okay if I help?"

She replies, "Yes, of course."

I sit down at the table and put the bank statements and cancelled checks in order. After 20 minutes of analyzing the documents and papers, I turn to her and say, "Well I finished reconciling your checkbook. I corrected an error. Your checkbook balance is actually $200 higher than you have recorded. So, it's an error correction that turns out to be in your favor."

She smiles and says, "What a relief! Thank you so much for your help."
"You're very welcome. I'm glad I could help."
I return to my classroom with a sense of satisfaction.

My mind snaps out of the day dream. Professor Judith is instructing the class on the proper use of ellipsis punctuation. I focus on her words as I re-enter my aspirational world of becoming a better writer.

Perhaps the opportunity for a retired accountant to be a hero will come another day.

Note: OLLI - Osher Lifelong Learning Institute at Furman University

PART 5

PROSE NON-FICTION

Summer 1960

Up until 1960 most summers in my life had a familiar rhythm to them. Every day revolved around playing baseball with my buddies at Branch Brook Park in Newark, followed by street stickball or whiffle ball games in the evening. The days almost always were closed out by the bells of the Good Humor truck that rolled down the street before dusk. My two-and-a-half-month ball playing season would be interrupted each year by a two-week vacation with my parents in Belmar, one of the busy summer towns on the Jersey Shore.

As I got a little older, street ball games and Good Humor trucks disappeared, but I still played baseball into my high school years. Summer vacations in Belmar continued as well. In the summer of 1960, however, there would be no Jersey Shore.

In August of that year my parents took me and my cousin, Gen Hopkins, on a two-week trip to Ireland. This was to be a mind opening experience. I had lived in Ireland for approximately a year at ages two and three, but had scant memory from that time.

Most of what I knew about Ireland came from stories of my parents and their relatives and friends who had emigrated from Ireland. But now, at age 16, I would have firsthand exposure to the land of their birth—an experience I *would* remember.

At that time, the flight on the TWA prop from Idlewild Airport to Shannon Airport in the west of Ireland took eleven hours. My father rented a car at Shannon and drove the four of us on a journey along two-lane country roads and through small towns until we reached the site of my mother's family home, Doocastle in County Mayo. The car journey lasted almost four hours. (A similar trip now would take two hours on the greatly improved road system.)

Warm embraces with smiles and tears were part of the greeting with Grandmother Bridget Hunt and Aunt Bea Hunt at the front door. We entered the house to the welcoming smell of turf burning in the fireplace, even though it was a summer day.

Afterwards my father and I walked out to the car to retrieve suitcases from the boot. As we emptied the car, a young boy about my age, wearing rough looking brown clothing, was walking up the road and approached us directly.

"A fag for me faether," he said.

My father ignored him.

"Kind sir, please, a fag for me faether."

My father replied, "Go on and get out of here."

He persisted, "It would be a kind man to give up a fag for me faether."

"I said get out of here."

He turned and walked away with a final comment, "Me faether likes kindness in a man."

My father explained to me that the boy was a tinker. Tinkers were families of gypsies who traveled in horse-drawn covered wagons. They tended to stay in areas for short periods of time, subsisting through varied means––doing odd jobs, begging for money, food, and other items, and in some cases, stealing. They rarely settled in one place for an extended period. Today, they are referred to as Travelers.

A few days later we spotted the boy and his family in a horse-drawn barrel shaped wagon, camped about a mile from Grandmother's house. They looked at us without expression, as they would the several other times we would pass them during our stay. The tinker boy never approached us again.

In addition to passing time on the Hunt farm with Grandmother and Aunt Bea, the initial days of our trip were spent visiting families my mother knew from her youth and traveling to a couple of local towns to see some small shops. I noticed on our drives that a local farmer on the road or a person standing on a sidewalk in town would wave hello to us. We would respond with a wave of our own. This happened often and was something new to me. People didn't wave hello to passing cars back in New Jersey.

One day Grandmother asked my parents if they would like to have chicken for supper and they responded affirmatively.

She turned to me and said, "Come with me, Joey."

I followed her out the backdoor into the adjoining yard and saw perhaps a dozen chickens scattered about. I had spent some time that morning day looking at these chickens walk about and peck at their food, and even had playfully chased them about for a time. I had never seen live chickens before.

Grandmother fixed her eyes on one of the birds and walked toward it. With a quickness that belied her stooped and aged appearance, her hand darted to grab the bird. She hoisted it in the air and twirled it twice, snapping its neck.

"This one will do nicely," she stated in a matter-of-fact manner.

She took the newly deceased bird into the house, cleaned it in preparation for boiling later, and set it aside. Up until that point in my life, every chicken I had seen had come in clear plastic wrapped packaging from the grocery store. Grandmother had given me a firsthand, mind opening, and appetite scuttling lesson in how the food chain really worked. I sat quietly during supper that evening picking tepidly at the dead bird with some degree of guilt. (See *Yard Work* elsewhere in this volume for a poetic account of this incident.)

The next day, a sunny windswept Thursday, we drove to visit my father's family in the small village of Glenavoo in County Sligo. The village adjoined Lough Talt in an idyllic setting at the base of the Ox Mountains. My father turned off the main road onto a narrow *boreen* lined with stone walls, scraping the side of the car at one point.

We reached the house and my father's brother, James Deehan, and his wife, Bridget Ann, came out to greet us with wide smiles. Upon entering the house, I met some of my young cousins. Uncle James then led us into an adjoining bedroom, where my father's mother lay bedridden, sitting against a propped-up pillow.

Upon seeing my father, she said in a weak voice, "It's my Joe."

My father sat on the side of the bed and they embraced tearfully. They had last seen each other 39 years earlier, when my father left Ireland at age

They chatted for a few minutes sharing joyful remembrances. My father introduced my mother, my cousin Gen, and me. Grandmother Bridget Deehan expressed happiness at finally meeting her grandson from America. The meeting with her did not last much longer as she began to tire. Two months later she would pass away at the age of 90.

I enjoyed connecting with my Deehan cousins in Glenavoo that day. These meetings opened an exciting realization of my having relatives close to my age I had never seen before.

Throughout the first week in Ireland, Gen and I spent all of our time visiting Hunt and Deehan relatives and friends and seeing various local sites with my parents. That was about to change.

John Ballantine was a city policeman in Newark. He was originally from Ireland and was visiting the country with his daughter, Catherine, at the same time as us. He knew my parents and had previously arranged to take Gen and me on a side trip to see other parts of Ireland.

John Ballantine had a strong interest in poetry and history, especially Irish history. With a calm, steady manner of speaking and a shock of white hair, he seemed to me more like a college professor than a policeman.

Mr. Ballantine was going to take Gen, Catherine, and me on a three-day trip to Dublin, Ireland's largest city. He picked Gen and me up at the Doocastle farm one morning and we headed off. After a stop for lunch at a pub in the town of Boyle, we made it to Dublin later that afternoon. We stayed at the historic Shelbourne Hotel near the city center.

Over the next two days we visited some famous and important Dublin sites. They included Trinity College, founded in 1591. A plethora of famous writers were educated at Trinity, including Oscar Wilde, Bram Stoker, Jonathan Swift, Samuel Beckett, Oliver Goldsmith and Thomas Moore. In the College's vast and historic library, we saw the Book of Kells, the world's most famous illuminated transcript of the Bible. I was impressed by the artistic detail laboriously created by the hands of monks more than a thousand years prior.

With Mr. Ballantine we also climbed the narrow steps of the160-foot Nelson's Pillar on O'Connell Street, Dublin's main thoroughfare. From the Pillar's viewing platform, we could see distant parts of low-rise Dublin in every direction. The arduous climb up those narrow winding steps was well worth the effort.

I didn't realize at the time the hatred that many Irish had for the Pillar, which was named after British naval hero Admiral Lord Nelson of Battle of Trafalgar fame. Six years later in 1966 the Pillar, along with Lord Nelson's statue, was blown up in a bombing attributed to the IRA. Today, a modernistic needle-like tower, the Spire of Dublin, almost three times the height of the original pillar, stands on that site. I saw the Spire on a visit to Dublin years later and frankly was more impressed with the Pillar.

On our return trip from Dublin to the Doocastle farm, we took a diversionary detour to a beautiful coastal spot outside the town of Sligo. We visited a small churchyard in Drumcliffe, where William Butler Yeats, a favorite poet of Mr. Ballantine, is buried. Mysterious poetic lines etched on Yeats' tombstone piqued my interest. (See the poem *Benbulben* in this volume.)

In my high school English class later that year, we would study Yeats' poem *The Lake Isle of Inisfree*. I took advantage of my visit to Yeats' gravesite to give my English teacher, John Ennis, a report on my stop there.

We spent the final few days of the trip at the Doocastle farm. One of the days was spent at work in the field with Aunt Bea, my parents, Gen, and neighbors from the area "saving the hay." Each summer the tall grass in the fields would be cut and left to dry for several days. Then the farmer, along with help from neighboring farmers (as was the custom), would manually rake and gather the hay into mounds or "reeks" as they were called. Today it is done by a mechanized process. Not so in 1960. Even though I was somewhat athletic at the time, my arms and shoulders ached quite a bit at the end of the day.

As they say, all good things come to an end. After two weeks, my parents, Gen and I left Ireland and returned to New Jersey. I became a city kid once again; but I had an advantage over my friends for they knew nothing about Yeats, Nelson's Pillar, tinkers, *processing* chickens, or "saving the hay."

* * *

I've had the opportunity to visit Ireland a number of times since that summer of 1960. I've seen a great deal of the country during those visits. My affinity for this country and its people has increased steadily as I've come to understand more about the essence of Ireland.

In 2013 my Aunt Bea Hunt died. She was the last survivor of my mother's family in Ireland. My Hopkins cousins in New Jersey and I inherited the Doocastle farm. We decided that because of our circumstances, it would not be practical to keep and manage it. So, with some reluctance we sold the farm, breaking a link to this land.

In 2014 I took my children and grandchildren to Ireland and brought them to see the sites of their Irish roots – the Hunt's Doocastle farm and the Deehan's Glenavoo homestead. I'm not sure how much of that connection was grasped by the grandchildren. I suspect it will likely have a stronger meaning for them when they grow a little older, as it did for me.

I also used the opportunity to take them to Yeats' gravesite in Drumcliffe, County Sligo. It stirred memory of my 1960 visit to the site. Many factors in life lead one to the interests they develop. Was Mr. Ballantine's diversionary side trip to Drumcliffe a factor leading to my interest in writing poetry, my retirement avocation? Perhaps.

Author and his family at former Hunt family home,
Doocastle, County Mayo, 2014

The Airplane Passenger

It was a bright sunny morning as the airplane lifted in a smooth takeoff from LAX. I was returning to Baltimore on a business flight. About an hour into the flight, I was reading and quite comfortable when I smelled smoke. Although this was in the 1980's when cigarette smoking was still permitted on commercial airplanes, as a former smoker I knew what I was smelling was not cigarette smoke. Having worked a decade earlier in midtown Manhattan across from Bryant Park, I recognized this scent as that of the same acrid, blue haze that would hang in the air, even at midday. I surmised what the source of this smell was.

I turned to look around, but in the wide first-class seat I couldn't see what was happening directly behind me. (Again, this was in the 1980's, when my employer still paid for first class airfare.) After a few moments the distinctive smell disappeared. I went back to my reading.

Shortly afterward a flight attendant began cabin service. I could sense movement from the person behind me. I saw a man walk past me in the aisle, headed toward the lavatory at the front of the cabin. The flight attendant slowly advanced the service cart forward in the aisle. She had stopped the cart to serve those in the seat row in front of me when the man returned from the lavatory. With the cart in the aisle, he had to stop and wait. He looked a bit unkempt with his hair tousled and about a three-day growth of beard stubble. He wore a rumpled shirt.

I initially didn't pay much attention to him, but thought he was the source of the suspect smoke. I looked again at him more closely. This time I realized I was looking directly at Jack Nicholson. I was surprised at his coarse appearance. Was he preparing for a movie role? Was this his normal public persona?

He returned my stare with a wry smirk. Did he know he had previously caught my attention?

After he got back to his seat, the rest of the flight was uneventful with no further smell of an illicit weed. We landed at O'Hare Airport where I was making a connection. The plane taxied to the gate. When the "all clear" sounded, I retrieved a case from the overhead compartment and walked toward the exit door. The first person waiting at the door was Nicholson. He had a fedora on and dark glasses. A young man behind him tried to engage him with some light banter but to no avail. Nicholson stayed focused on the door without comment and as soon as it was opened, he walked quickly up the jetway and disappeared among the throng of travelers.

The following evening, I was at home watching the NBA playoff game between the Lakers and the Celtics in Boston. At one point in the game the television camera panned the fans in Boston Garden and stopped to focus on Jack Nicholson sitting courtside. He was after all a rabid fan of the Lakers. He was clean shaven with hair combed neatly, wearing a stylish floral print shirt.

After a brief moment, Nicholson turned and his focus was toward the camera. As he looked directly at me, a wry smile appeared on his face. It was as if from 400 miles away, he was letting me know he knew that I knew about his inflight smoking and that he didn't care. He seemed to be instructing me on the weight of celebrity status.

The Power of Inference

October 31, 1951, 6:15pm
The Deehan Apartment, 105 North 9th Street,
Newark, New Jersey

Joe Deehan and Mary Deehan with their son, Joey, are seated in the small kitchen of their apartment having supper.

Mary says, "Joey, how was school today?"

Joey, who seems preoccupied moving peas around his plate with a fork, replies, "Good."

Joe interjects, "So, how was your Halloween party?"

"It was fun."

Mary says, "Joey, tell us more about it."

"All the kids wore their costumes. There was one other clown, Billy Dunn. Except he didn't have a red, plastic nose like mine. Some kids were cowboys."

"What did the girls dress as?"

"Oh, I dunno...princesses and stuff like that."

"That's nice. Did Sister Theresa have any Halloween treats?"

"Yeah, there was candy and cookies and stuff...and juice."

Mary replies, "It sounds like you had a good time at your party."

"Yeah, I did Mommy. Oh, I forgot. Sister Theresa said we still had a lot of candy and stuff left. She said we'd finish the Halloween party tomorrow. So, I'll wear my clown costume again tomorrow."

Joe looks at his son with uncertainty. "Are you sure you're supposed to wear your costume again?"

"Yeah, Daddy. She said we'd finish the party tomorrow. So we have to have our costumes on for that."

"Okay Joey. Well, you'll have more fun tomorrow."

November 1, 8:25am

Two blocks from his apartment, Joey walks through the school yard adjacent to St. Rose of Lima School, the place where the students assemble by class and walk in pairs into the school building. As he walks past the second and third-grade assemblies, several of the students start laughing and jeering.

"Hey kid, did you forget what day it is?"

Another voice sounds, "Do you work for the circus, kid?"

Joey thinks they just don't know his class is having another Halloween party today. He continues walking and sees his classmates ahead. He freezes with fear. None of them are wearing their Halloween costumes. Sister Theresa is giving her normal directives, telling the students to assemble in boy-girl rows of two. She stares at Joey for a moment but continues her assembly instructions.

Amid laughs and giggles from his classmates, Joey removes his red nose and proceeds to his normal spot next to Maureen Reilly. She has her eyes straight ahead, not acknowledging his presence. As they start their march into the school, it's not apparent which of the two is more embarrassed...Joey, the clown, or Maureen, the assembly partner of the clown.

As the students enter the classroom, Sister Theresa brings Joey over to her side and, while bending down, whispers in a non-threatening tone, "Joseph, why are you wearing your clown costume today?'

Joey, his knees shaking, replies, "You told us, Sister, we'd finish our Halloween candy and stuff today. I thought we had to wear our costume."

"No, Joseph. I never said that and I didn't mean that."

"I'm sorry, Sister."

"That's all right, Joseph. Do you have clothes under your costume?"

"Yes, Sister. I have dungarees and an undershirt."

"Then just take off your costume and go to your seat."

"Yes, Sister."

Joey removes his clown suit and takes his seat, trying to shrink and make himself as small as possible. When Sister Theresa later allows the class to go to the back of the room and have leftover candy and cookies, Joey remains fixed in his seat, seeking invisibility. In the depths of mortification, he does not want to stand with his dingy clothes in contrast to the other boys with their white shirts and ties. He prays no one will look at him for the rest of the day...the day he truly has become the *class clown*.

That evening Joey recounts the story of his day to his parents and begins to cry. His mother consoles him, saying "Don't cry, Joey. It was an honest mistake. Sister Theresa wasn't mad at you. She knows it was just a mistake. You'll feel better tomorrow and someday you'll be able to look back and laugh about it."

* * *

Seven decades later

My mother was right that evening. Today, I do look back and laugh about a childhood incident forever imbedded in my mind. Perhaps, others can muster a chuckle as well.

The Concert

I was looking forward to the evening with my friends, Richie Lorenzo and Joe Higgins. They pulled up in front of my house around 6:00pm. After a quick goodbye to my parents, I hopped in the back of Joe's convertible and we were on our way to Forest Hills. We left Newark and soon found ourselves in heavy congestion on the Route 3 approach to the Lincoln Tunnel. Despite the many times I had made this crossing, I had always felt anxiety being in a tunnel under the Hudson River. I had a habit of focusing on the ceiling of the tunnel to look for drops of water that would signal my impending doom. Of course, the mighty river never did crash down on me.

After tortoise-like travel through midtown Manhattan, we crossed into Queens and soon found our way to the neighborhood of Forest Hills. We parked on a residential street and walked several blocks to Forest Hills Stadium. The venue was famous as the site for many historic United States Open tennis championships.

Little did the three of us know that the concert we were headed to would achieve its own historical status in the annals of rock and roll.

I knew Bob Dylan songs before I had ever heard of Bob Dylan. Peter, Paul and Mary had a hit folk song with "Blowin' in the Wind" in 1963. It reached number two on the Billboard pop chart. It had become an anthem of the civil rights movement. Another of their releases, "Don't Think Twice, It's Alright," reached number nine. In early 1965 The Byrds had a hit record with Dylan's "Mr. Tambourine Man." I was fascinated with the sound and the mystical, poetic lyrics of the song. (To this day I can still get absorbed in those lyrics.) A bit later The Turtles covered another Dylan song, "It Ain't Me Babe." Rock and Roll artists were starting to turn his folk songs into Top 40 hits.

I became a big fan of Bob Dylan and purchased all his early albums. (Do you remember 33 1/3 vinyl records?) In the summer of 1965 Dylan had a huge hit with the release of "Like a Rolling Stone." The song contained lyrics with a deep message about the human condition and the turn of fortune one can face in life. It also had a strong rock and roll sound with electric guitars, organ and drums. Dylan's folk purist fans believed fervently that the wonder of electricity should have no association with music and hoped this was just a one-off experiment on his part. (In 2003 *Rolling Stone Magazine* ranked this as the top rock and roll song of all time.)

On that August night in 1965, two types of Dylan fans filled the stadium––the folk purists and those who, like myself, appreciated both the folk songs and the newer rock sounds in his music. The concert opened with Dylan walking onto the stage dressed in black with an acoustic guitar and a harmonica set in a holder resting on his shoulders. He sang seven songs including "Desolation Row" and "Mr. Tambourine Man." Each song received enthusiastic applause from the audience. It was a solid opening set followed by a short intermission.

Things would be different in the second set. Dylan reappeared on stage with an electric guitar accompanied by Robbie Robertson, Levon Helm and other musicians replete with electric guitars, electric keyboard and drums. (This group would later become well known in its own right as The Band.) From the opening note of the set, cat calls and boos started to erupt from parts of the audience. The purists were taking offense at every electronic chord and every pounding drum beat.

But Dylan played on.

The set was comprised of eight songs, including "Like a Rolling Stone" and "Ballad of a Thin Man." Each song had a definitive rock sound. Several times the most rabid of the purists tried to disrupt the concert by throwing various objects at the stage and even rushing it. But they were unsuccessful in attempts to halt the music.

Dylan played on.

The minority purists were loud and obnoxious and set a nervous edge around the concert. But Dylan completed the set as he had planned and, in contrast with the negativity, received supportive applause from the semi-quiet majority.

My friends and I enjoyed the concert that night and were left bemused by the vociferous critics. Richie commented that Dylan's dual persona performance and the audience reaction would make it a memorable event. None of us realized, however, the iconic nature of what we had just witnessed. This was the initial concert in a tour that Dylan continued across the United States over the remainder of 1965 and brought to England in 1966. He received similar raucous responses from audiences at each venue but never wavered. Robbie Robertson, who played back up to Dylan at every tour venue, provides an interesting account of the experience in his autobiography, "Testimony".

Dylan's mixture of folk music and rock and roll was here to stay and came to be known as folk rock. Rock and roll was to be transformed from a medium for conveying simplistic lyrics of teenage love to one that could explore the broad gamut of human experience. The Beatles and the Rolling Stones would be among the scores of musical groups to be influenced by Dylan and both started recording *message* songs. Martin Scorsese would reference the Forest Hills concert years later in his documentary about Dylan, "Don't Look Back".

My strong interest in Dylan continued. I bought all of his albums in the 1960's and early 1970's. Thereafter, family and career became priorities and I didn't follow Dylan as closely as before. In 2016 Dylan was awarded the Nobel Prize for Literature, the first songwriter to win the award. This rekindled my Dylan interest. One morning I awoke with a few poetic lines in my head. In two hours, I wrote the first draft of what would become my Bob Dylan poem, titled

Hibbing, MN, which is the town where Dylan grew up. I would later include this in my published book of poetry, "Solar Reflection". Of course, on that long ago August 1965 night, I had no idea I would one day publish a poem about the poetic songwriter who set a new musical tone for his generation.

Hibbing, MN

He grew up in Hibbing town,
kept his ear low to the ground.
Quiet place old Hibbing town.
The young man left to release his sound.
"*It's Alright Ma.*"

Outside the town, his freedom found,
soon success in New York and Newport town
with harmonica and acoustic sounds.
"*Hey Mr. Tambourine Man, play a song for me.*"

From folk to rock, exploration unwound,
he went electric, to some *a complete unknown,*

"*Like a Rolling Stone.*"
The dogs barked and yelped inside the pound.
JUDAS! BETRAYAL! DON'T CONFOUND!
"*Positively 4th Street.*" He put them down.

But the sound it spread and would resound.
In time he achieved world renown,
some 700 songs, the words abound.
The world is now his music crown
and Nobel sits atop that crown,
a poet true within his sound.
"*Forever Young.*"

They're feeling down in Hibbing town,
couldn't foresee the boy would astound
planet Earth with words profound.
Throughout downtown they wear a frown
'cause Bobby left and don't come 'round.
"*It's All Over Now Baby Blue.*"

Poem - J. Deehan 2017
Italics – Bob Dylan

The Thanksgiving Day Race

Uncle Tim, Aunt Helen and my cousins arrived for our annual Thanksgiving get-together. I expected it to be the usual warm and fuzzy family gathering. I did not anticipate the athletic competition that would become part of family lore.

My parents owned a three-story brick house in the Roseville section of Newark, New Jersey. They rented out the top two floors. Since I was an only child, the three of us fit comfortably into the four rooms of the ground floor. The living room converted into my bedroom at night through the magic of a sleeper sofa. Each year the living room also served as a dining room for the Thanksgiving feast with the use of a large folding table covered by Mom's Irish linen tablecloth and set with her annually-used china and silverware.

Aunt Helen and my older cousins, Jo and Helen, helped Mom in the kitchen with the dinner preparation while Uncle Tim held court in the living room with Jo's husband Paul, cousins Gen and Kay, Dad and me. As was the norm, his strong views on politics, union labor matters, sports and life in general dominated the conversation.

At five o'clock Mom announced that the food was ready. Dad carried in the large platter of carved turkey, followed by my aunt and cousins with companion dishes of mashed potatoes, stuffing, green bean casserole, cranberry sauce, biscuits and gravy. With everyone seated, Dad offered the blessing and the food dishes began their carousel around the table. The meal was supplemented with stories and banter about neighbors and friends, the parish and events in Roseville.

The Thanksgiving meal experience left a comfortable afterglow in the conversation...that is, for the most part. At one point I must have said something dealing with my high school athletics. I don't recall exactly what it was; but it prompted Uncle Tim, who liked to throw playful digs my way, to interject in his County Mayo accent.

"You know, Joey, you might think you are fast, but I could outrun you."

I laughed with derision and said, "There's no way you could outrun me."

Not willing to leave it there, he replied, "I'll bet you that I can beat you running, let's say in a race around the block."

"I'll race you anytime you want."

"Okay. I'll bet you one dollar that I can beat you in a race that starts in front of your house, goes down to Sixth Avenue, then left to Roseville Avenue, to Seventh Avenue and back to the finish at the house."

"I'll do that."

The challenge was on. We were going to race that night, after the table was cleared but before dessert was served. We agreed to wait one-half hour to allow dinner to settle. I eagerly looked forward to the race knowing I would beat Uncle Tim easily and perhaps keep him subdued and quiet for a while. After all I was sixteen, an athlete; and he was in his mid-fifties with a penchant for his ever-present Chesterfield cigarettes.

Around seven o'clock we started in front of the house with Dad, Paul and the cousins looking on. I broke into an energetic pace while Uncle Tim took a slow jog approach.

I reached the first turn at Sixth Avenue and looking back saw him some 50 yards behind. Running the short block to Roseville Avenue I looked back again but he was not in sight. I ran up Roseville Avenue, normally a busy street. There was not a moving car or a person in sight, including Uncle Tim, on this cold November night. Reaching the next turn with still no sign of my fifty-something competitor, I started to contemplate how much fun I would have at home mocking his flawed challenge.

I reached home and no one was outside. I eagerly climbed the steps to make my triumphant entry. Surely none would be surprised. I walked into the living room and there sat Uncle Tim with a Cheshire Cat grin on his face.

"What took you so long? I finished a few minutes ago," he said.

I was stunned. What happened? This wasn't possible. Did he cut through a yard and hop a fence?

He broke into laughter as did everyone else in the room.

I yelled, "This can't be. You were never even close to me."

He continued to laugh and then, feigning seriousness, said, "Now don't be a sore loser, Joey. You lost, so you have to pay up."

My cousins continued to laugh at me. I finally realized what had happened. I had never seen him after the first turn. After I left his sight, he stopped and turned around, and simply walked back to the house, probably laughing all the way…as I continued to run.

I had been duped by my uncle, who played me using the lure of my athlete ego.

The laughter of the group at my plight went on. I could tell there was no hope of turning the tide with my claim of fraud. He finally *forgave* my debt saying he felt sorry for me.

The family gathering ended that day with all on good terms, although I remained a bit irked. There were to be no future athletic competitions within our family. Uncle Tim, however, would not hesitate to remind me of his Thanksgiving Day victory, whenever he thought a gentle jab to my ego would be appropriate.

To Forgive Is Divine

The sun shone brightly over the vast crowd on a May 1981 afternoon. Anticipation built as some ten thousand awaited his arrival, hoping to catch a glimpse of the humble Polish priest who in the early years of his Papacy was already influencing world events.

The din of voices and cheers arose at the far end of the square indicating his arrival. The noise grew louder as he slowly made his way through the throng. Suddenly four shots sounded generating an eruption of screams and yelling. He slumped in the open-air vehicle as aides rushed to help him. Others nearby quickly pounced on the would-be assassin.

Pope John Paul II lay gravely wounded in the rear of the vehicle. All four shots had found their target. Two bullets had entered his lower intestine, one had hit his right arm and the fourth had hit a finger. Two bystanders—a 60-year-old woman from Buffalo, New York and a 23-year-old Jamaican woman—were also wounded. (They both later recovered from their wounds.)

The Pope was rushed to Rome's Gemeli Hospital where he underwent five hours of surgery. He had suffered great loss of blood and two sections of his intestine had to be removed. That evening his condition was listed as critical, but stable.

* * *

Mehmet Ali Agca belonged to a Turkish terrorist group called Gray Wolves. The group had been responsible for numerous political assassinations in Turkey in the 1970's. In February 1979 Agca had been arrested and charged with the murder of a Turkish newspaper editor. While awaiting trial, he escaped from a military prison in November 1979. In his cell he left a letter stating he would shoot the Pope and referred to him as "the Crusader Commander John Paul under the mask of a religious leader." A Turkish court later convicted Agca of the newspaper editor murder in absentia.

* * *

John Paul II's recovery was steady, but due to the severity of his wounds he had to remain in Gemeli Hospital for three weeks. Only four days after being shot, however, John Paul asked for all Catholics to "pray for my brother (Agca)...whom I have sincerely forgiven." His statement was soon known throughout the world. Many people, including myself, were amazed at this message directed at the man who had just tried to kill him.

Before too long, John Paul II made a full recovery and resumed a busy schedule of mission, prayer, love and forgiveness that would last through most of his remaining life. He would go onto to visit more countries and be seen by more people worldwide than any other pope in history. I had the privilege of seeing him in person in Baltimore in October 1995.

Images of John Paul II with people of all races and ages throughout the world are innumerable. He exuded warmth in his contacts with people and seemed to be comfortable with those from any station in life.

One image stands out in my mind above all others. On December 28, 1983, John Paul II visited Mehmet Ali Agca in Rome's Rebibbia Prison. Agca had been sentenced to life in prison by an Italian court. On that day John Paul sat and talked with Agca in his cell without others present. There is no record of what was said between them. A photo shows the two of them seated alone, John Paul with his head bent toward Agca, no more than two feet away, and Agca with his eyes fixed attentively on the Pope. My inference from that image is that John Paul was offering comfort to Agca. In 1987 the Pope would meet with Agca's mother and, some years later, his brother.

Agca had been sentenced to life imprisonment, but in 2000 Pope John Paul II suggested that he be pardoned. The Pontiff had declared 2000 to be a Great Jubilee Year in which the cornerstone was to be forgiveness. Italian President Carlo Azeglio Ciampi pardoned Agca in 2000 and he was extradited to Turkey where he was imprisoned for his 1979 murder of the newspaper editor. Agca was released from prison in January 2010 after almost three decades of imprisonment.

* * *

John Paul II died on April 2, 2005. He endured declining health in the last few years of his life. It is suspected he suffered from Parkinson's Disease near the end of his life but that was never officially confirmed. In 2014 he was canonized a saint by the Catholic Church.

Mehmet Ali Agca visited the Vatican in 2014. He spent several moments standing at the tomb of the late Pontiff before laying two bunches of white roses at the site. It is reported that Agca now lives a quiet life in Turkey caring for rescue cats.

* * *

Saint John Paul II lived a remarkable life. He spent his youth growing up in Poland, a country wedged between the ever-increasing threats of Nazi Germany and Communist Russia. In later life, he became one of the most influential leaders of the late twentieth century. As great as his world achievements may have been, his forgiveness of the man who almost took his life stands out as a singular act of courage and compassion, one that stays etched in my mind.

John Paul II visiting Mehmet Ali Agca in Agca's prison cell on December 28, 1983

www.ingramcontent.com/pod-product-compliance
Lightning Source LLC
LaVergne TN
LVHW061624070526
838199LV00070B/6565